Research Project Planning

A Comprehensive Guide for Non-Experimental Research in the Health Professions

Research Project Planning

A Comprehensive Guide for Non-Experimental Research in the Health Professions

---

Embraceable Goals, Achievable Results

---

dès Anges Cruser, PhD, MPA

Foreword by Jim Frost, MS

Commercial Publication - By Time: Life of Publication

Purpose: Uses where the cartoon will be part of a publication (not the cover) made available to people outside the purchasing organization. This includes all print publishing uses where the image is part of the editorial content of the publication and will be used at half page size or smaller. Also covers use in catalogues or brochures sold, taking paying advertising, or used in the promotion of a commercial entity. All Commercial Publication licenses include electronic rights.

Edited by Kim Carr.
KimsOnTheMark.com

Cover Design and typesetting by Lucy Holtsnider.
LucyHoltsnider.com/Book-Design

ISBN 978-1-7362916-0-3

Dedication

This work is dedicated to health professions students and practitioners everywhere. At every stage of your life-long learning journey, I encourage you to ask questions and keep seeking knowledge for the betterment of all.

This book would not have been created without the lessons I learned from my students. Thank you all.

Nor would this book have been finished without the encouragement of my introspective husband and brilliant colleague, Alan Lee Podawiltz, DO, MS, FAPA.

Introduction and Overview

Welcome to your research project!

I'm guessing you have this book because you have to do a research study or a scholarly project. Perhaps this is not necessarily your cup of tea, so to speak. Your focus, as a healthcare student or practitioner, is on improving the lives of your patients and clients. You have a lot on your plate. You want to be the best possible healthcare provider in your field. Appropriately, that is your current all-consuming goal. So, a research project is likely a requirement to complete your program of study. You can do this!

Between a general idea for a research project and a solid, measurable study question or aim, and between that question and the data collection and analyses, there are many hurdles to clear. To clear those hurdles, you need suitable tools. These tools include a game plan, a roadmap, and specific skills and abilities, and knowledge. Trust me, the challenges you face at this moment can be overcome. With the right tools, you will arrive at the finish line, having met your project goals.

This book can be used at any stage of academic and professional training, from undergraduate to graduate to postgraduate studies. Practicum students, interns and residents, and post-doc trainees who don't plan to pursue a research career can also use this book to their advantage. By acquiring this comprehensive guide to research

project planning, you've jumped the first hurdle toward creating and organizing your research project.

This guide has thirteen chapters and three appendices. Each chapter is divided into subsections of related topics. Before the table of contents, I've provided a brief summary of the contents of each chapter.

Now for a word from my good friend and colleague Jim Frost, MS.

Foreword

Greetings! I'm Jim Frost, MS. I'm an experienced teacher, data analyst and statistical communicator. I've published several books on understanding statistics, and I'd like to tell you why I think you've picked the right book to jump-start your research project.

In one of my books, *Introduction to Statistics,* I used an intuitive approach to help novice researchers understand statistical tools and their power to reveal meaning in their data. I dedicated an entire chapter to the process of designing a scientifically rigorous study. But my colleague, des Anges Cruser, dedicates this entire book to that process. Her book is a detailed, step-by-step instructional manual on how to construct a strong non-experimental health sciences research project plan.

While my focus has been primarily on experimental and quasi-experimental research, foundational statistical principles apply to non-experimental research as well. In experimental research, the main question is whether a specified action causes a hypothesized outcome; whereas in non-experimental research, the researcher is asking whether there is a relationship between an observed condition and an outcome.

As a reviewer and a contributor to des Anges' book, I can recommend it as an essential tool for improving the trustworthiness of your statistical analysis. Statistics are keys that unlock hidden meaning in the data. Thus, any results from statistical tests are less likely to be valid if data come from a poorly planned study. First, you need to have a complete project plan, then you can collect relevant data, and finally, you will perform appropriate analyses. This guide to research project planning, and its companion workbook are the foundations for a well-planned study.

While research and statistics may be inseparable, they don't need to be insufferable. We can't just talk randomly about statistics (pardon the pun); statistics is all about content and context. So is planning your project. Using her impressive experience with research and teaching as an associate professor of medical education, des Anges can help you conquer the inevitable challenges inherent in research project planning.

The health sciences constantly roil with some of the most intriguing unanswered questions. Every healthcare field has phenomena begging to be explored. Although you might think that experimental research is the only credible type of scientific exploration, nonexperimental research has remarkable power to expand human scientific knowledge. A powerful example of this can be found in a 1973 article published in the British medical journal, *The Lancet,* in which researchers established the clinical construct for Fetal Alcohol Syndrome. Using non-experimental research methods, scientists identified an irrefutable relationship between alcohol consumption during pregnancy and irreversible pre-natal neurological damage.

It is important to keep in mind that a carefully composed research question determines the pathway to discovery. As I say in my book, "Discovery is a bumpy road." So how do you proceed? My suggestion is to let des Anges walk you through the process.

If planning a research project seems impossible, you will soon feel more confident with the information and tools in this book. Each chapter lays out manageable tasks for organizing the building blocks in each section of a complete and scientifically sound research project plan. As a bonus, there are electronic templates for entering information that will populate each plan section, as well as fuel essential discussions with advisors and statisticians.

As I reviewed this book, it felt like des Anges was there with me, sharing her experience, wisdom, and vital information for each step of the process! I think you'll find that you can design a project that will successfully expand our understanding of health status and healthcare. That's exciting!

Overview of Chapters

Chapter One. *Introduction and Overview* talks about the journey of research and how to create and use a roadmap to reach your goals. It offers guidance on how to use this book to your best advantage.

Chapter Two. *What to know before you begin.* In this chapter, you'll find information on the most commonly used non-experimental research designs in health-related fields, education, and social sciences. You'll also find five other project structures briefly described that are suited for students or beginning researchers in the healthcare professions. It provides checklists for determining the feasibility of your project, tasks and strategies you should employ, and skills and abilities you need and how to evaluate them.

Chapter Three. *The Research Project Plan* provides an orientation to the purpose of a plan and the three major sections. It includes an outline of a project plan, so you have a general idea of what constitutes each section before you dive into writing and learning how each part connects to form a whole project plan.

Chapter Four. *The Study Question* takes you through the process of developing your study question, including all necessary considerations for making it measurable. It covers defining the study variables as well as considerations for data availability and access.

Chapter Five. *The Literature Search,* and its Relationship to the Other Plan Sections, provides guidance on preparing for and conducting a literature search efficiently and thoroughly. It covers how to evaluate the articles or other source material in depth, critically, and creatively. It gives you tools for organizing the information and how the information pertains to and is used in each section of the project plan.

Chapter Six. *Background & Importance Section* takes you through the process of constructing and writing a review of the literature, and how it pertains to and supports the rationale for your project.

Chapter Seven. *Structure & Methods Section* takes you through the process of constructing and writing the narrative that describes the project design, study subjects, sampling, and the steps you will take in collecting and analyzing data. It covers how you plan to manage all the tasks needed to conduct and complete the project.

Chapter Eight. *Data Management* gives you an orientation to data collection, data entry, and data analysis issues. You need a conversational knowledge of statistics for any scholarly project.

I've provided some guidance on how acquire that knowledge as well as several sources for you to find trustworthy, basic information on statistical tests.

Chapter Nine. Specific Aims Section takes you through the process of constructing and writing your Executive Summary.

Chapter Ten. Review Chapter brings you full circle to the complete project plan. You'll review your progress, revisit your templates, and complete a master plan for your project.

Chapter Eleven. Other Types of Research Projects describes and provides guidance on case studies, a focused review of the literature, survey research, field & observational, and exploratory studies. Some of these may be used to develop questionnaires and scales. This chapter discusses the process, the challenges, the benefits, and the opportunities with these types of projects.

Chapter Twelve. Scientific Writing provides guidance on writing clearly for the project plan in your reports and findings.

Chapter Thirteen. Human Subjects Protections and the Institutional Review Board (IRB), contains guidance on protection of human subjects' information, consents, and the institutional review board.

Appendix 1. Terminology, Study Designs & Project Structures, has two sections. Section A. Research Concepts and Terminology contains brief definitions of the most commonly used terms in non-experimental research, with references to additional resources for expanded definitions. Section B provides definitions of the four most common research designs and five other project structures for non-experimental research. I've kept a focus on modest-sized projects. Knowing the different study designs will help you decide what would be a reasonable size and scope for your situation and your research question.

Appendix 2.   *Resources,* contains resources and citations.

Appendix 3.   *Templates* and links to download fillable forms for constructing your project plan.

A research study is a significant investment of your time, energy, and intellectual capital.

Try to develop a project that is realistic, but at the same time do not limit yourself by what you think might be problems or obstacles.

Always look for a way to accomplish your goals. Come on, now, let's think out of the box, and picture you successful!

Table of Contents

ONE

The Research Journey

What to Expect

I've conducted a lot of research in psychology, in medicine, on leadership, and in education. I've also advised hundreds of students, interns, and residents in various healthcare professions in creating and conducting their scholarly research projects. I've taught graduate students and residents the principles of clinical research, reviewed and edited thousands of proposals and papers, and published numerous articles. I've rolled all my experience into this book to help you conquer the tasks before you—easily, smoothly, and successfully.

My experience with students and novice researchers has taught me many lessons. I've learned how chaotic research projects feel to them, and I've developed tools to simplify the process. I've seen paralyzing anxiety over a research project because of statistics, and I've provided guidance on how to communicate with a statistics advisor.

While research and statistics are not the same constructs, you will need to have an understanding of how they are related. As a healthcare professional, you'll want to understand the statistics underlying evidence-based practice guidelines. As a healthcare professions student conducting a small research project, you only need knowledge of the stats that apply to your data, and there are many ways to meet that need.

If statistics make your head spin, there are some resources I recommend to help stop that spinning. The first set of resources is by my statistics contributor and colleague, Jim Frost. His website is: *https://statisticsbyjim.com/.* There you will find several books on statistics that Jim has written in plain language. They are organized in a way that makes it easy to understand terminology, explore examples of statistical analysis methods, and find answers to your questions. Another valuable resource is *Intuitive Biostatistics: A Nonmathematical Guide to Statistical Thinking* by Harvey Motulsky. These resources will help you in ways you that will amaze you.

You know by now that this Research Project Planning Guide is not about statistics. It is all about helping you to create a feasible project, access additional resources, and work with others essential to your success. Working with others is part of the project planning process. Advisors can answer questions, but they can't do more unless you tell them what you need. Communication is essential. The tools in this guide can be used to facilitate meaningful discussions with your advisors, using your completed templates.

As you work through this guide, remember that conducting a research study has the added benefit of sharpening your thinking skills. Constructing and completing a scholarly project will strengthen your competencies in identifying, collecting, and analyzing information to answer a question. And one more thing. It showcases your ability to communicate with others about your findings or results.

Research is problem solving.

It's what you do to get answers.

To buy groceries, you scan the shelves, read labels, consult your recipes, or get in touch with your "what-sounds-good-for-dinner" meter.

To buy a car, you look at multiple body styles and horsepower—or maybe not that one—colors, MPG, and prices. You match your needs (kids? dogs? luggage? sports equipment?) with the style and size vehicle that meets them.

Research is results oriented.

It's what you do to get results.

This book is for you if…

- You are a student, intern, or post-doctoral trainee or novice researcher in a health-related field.
- You are conducting a non-experimental research or scholarly project in an English-speaking community.
- Your resources and time are both limited.
- You will use existing (free or purchased) data or collect data from sources you are authorized to access, using a free or licensed test of knowledge, a survey, or a questionnaire, or your own data collection forms.
- You have an advisor, a biostatistician, and colleagues with

whom you must or can discuss your project and/or may collaborate.
- Your project uses data subject to review under human subjects' protection rules and regulations.
- You have or will independently acquire a competence in statistics and human subjects' protection sufficient to complete your project.

How does this guide make your path easier?

This book will help you to organize the steps involved in constructing and conducting your project.

First, it provides easy to understand descriptions of non-experimental research designs and other project structures.

Second, it gives you both a high-level overview of the sections of a research project plan and their essential elements as well as detailed, step-by-step instructions with fillable templates for constructing each section.

Third, it includes guidance on meeting with your advisors, determining your local research requirements, and addressing data management and human subjects' protection concerns.

Structure of the Research Project Plan

In the United States, grant applications for funding from the federal government, and many other national and local granting organizations, must follow certain guidelines for content and integrity. A research project plan has the same core elements that are in a grant proposal: an introduction that presents the aim or goal of the project and a summary of the other core sections, a review of relevant literature, a description of the structure and methods to be used to conduct the study, and all required human subjects' protection elements.

The contents of this book are aligned with the guidelines used by National Institutes of Health (the NIH) for research grant proposals. Although a research project plan is not a grant application, many of the same core elements apply.

Over the years, the NIH has modified its guidelines and requirements. Their instructions have become more consistent and easier to locate and follow. As of the year 2020, the NIH guidelines call for two main sections in a grant proposal: "Specific Aims" and "Research Strategy," each with specified elements depending on the type of proposal. Under "Research Strategy," there are three subheadings: "Significance," "Innovation," and "Approach." Other sections include resources, human subjects, or other elements of research protocol, rules, and law.

I have not used the same terminology as the NIH, because this book is for creating a plan of action, not a grant application, and it is for non-experimental designs that do not require extensive methodology sections. I do, however, adhere to the principles of that gold standard, while clarifying terminology for the novice researcher. I've incorporated the lessons I learned from being a student of research, from publishing findings from my own studies, and from guiding non-research track students, graduates, and post-doctoral trainees through their research projects.

You can label sections many different ways. In fact, your institution may have its own outline. If that is the case, the material and templates in this book can be used to populate any outline. All the necessary pieces are here.

What is important is that you understand what the section headings mean and what elements must be covered in each one. As a novice researcher you need to know how to construct each section of a research project plan and how to connect them to produce one coherent document. That document can serve a dual purpose: as a proposal to get approval from an advisor or institution, and as a plan for conducting the project.

The four headings I use are: "Specific Aims" (the executive summary and introduction), "Background & Importance" (review of relevant literature/source material, how it supports the rationale for the project, and its value to the field), "Structure & Methods" (project design/approach, data collection and management, and project tasks), and "Human Subjects Protections" (as required).

The order in which required information is presented may vary by institution or instructor, but the core elements of a solid and complete research project plan remain the same. I also provide guidance on the human subject protections elements required in proposals dealing with personal health information or identifiers.

One more thing: I use the terms research project, scholarly project, and study interchangeably throughout this book. All of these are grounded in the scientific method of observing, measuring, examining, and formulating conclusions, without the experiment or manipulation step.

What will this book help me to do?

The tools in this guide enable you to create material you can use to populate any outline. I have used the words "project" and "study" interchangeably throughout the book. Regardless of the type of project you are doing, the focus is on constructing the plan you'll use to conduct and complete it. The term "data" throughout the book applies to any information you collect to address your study question.

Using the guide and the templates, you will be able to accomplish the following tasks to construct a feasible project plan.

- Evaluate the feasibility of your project.
- Identify those with whom you should discuss your project and how that works.
- Create a measurable research question.
- Identify the most appropriate research design or project structure for your project.
- Prepare for and conduct an organized, useful literature search.
- Write the Background & Importance narrative.
- Identify and define study variables.
- Organize the data acquisition, collection, management, and analysis processes.
- Write the Structure & Methods section of the plan.
- Attend appropriately to human subjects research rules and regulations.

With this guide and its templates, you will become more confident about:
✓ What you are going to do,
✓ Why you are going to do it,
✓ How you will do it,
✓ What you will use to do it, and
✓ How long it will take you to finish.

TWO

What to Know Before You Begin

Overview

Before you begin your project, you should be familiar with all requirements or conditions your institution or coursework has governing research projects.

The material in this book applies to non-experimental research projects. Non-experimental designs do not have an intervention or treatment. There is no attempt to change an outcome or manipulate a variable. However, depending on the study scope and size, a non-experimental project could consume as many resources, and be as complex as, an experimental study. The material in this book attends primarily to small-to-medium sized projects that are temporally brief and rely on few resources.

What do you need to know before diving into creating a project plan?

Research has a language you need to understand. It is essential that you recognize certain concepts and terminology and use them appropriately. In *Appendix 1. Terminology, Study Designs & Project Structures*, you will find definitions, examples, discussion points, and cautions for twenty research terms and concepts. While you don't need to memorize them, you should read research articles with this (or another) glossary of terms at hand. Practice is the way to learn what these mean and how to use them.

Be careful where you get your definitions. As a caution, please be aware that searching out research terminology and concepts on the internet is a mixed bag of delight and devastation. Some sources are clear and helpful, some are too complicated for your purposes, and some are confusing or misleading. I use the simplest possible definitions, in plain language. You can find more detailed definitions and discussions online or in a more in-depth research textbook. Appendix 2 provides a list of resources.

Non-experimental research has historically gotten a bad rap. Experimental research is still the way medical breakthroughs and advances occur. It is rigorously designed and governed, and nearly impossible to conduct and complete without financing.

Experimental studies are intensive in their structure, regulated in their methodologies, and highly statistically driven.

For your purposes, as a novice researcher, a non-research track student, or postgraduate trainee, a research project that is non-experimental (non-e), is robust enough. Perhaps one could say that it is the journey through the project that is more important than the end result. (But keep that end result in mind anyway!)

A non-e scholarly project will improve your analytic and critical thinking skills, both of which are underpinnings of your clinical skills.

For decades, research designs have been traditionally and rigidly defined because the question and the data in a study determine the design and the statistical tests appropriate to the type of data being analyzed. Scholarly projects and non-experimental research designs are more flexible in their structure and methods than experimental designs. With that said, it should be noted that a scholarly project may be equally demanding as they challenge a student researcher to think critically about information in the broad context of a profession. You will still use the scientific method of discovery.

Some research designs are "more intense" than others; they require more resources or study subjects or cases. When you know the different types of research designs and other project structures, you are be better prepared to craft your study question in a way that fits the capacity of your available resources and time.

The process of formulating a complete research project plan is an iterative process. That means you will go through repeated cycles of constructing materials, reviewing them, and revising them, before you have a final project all mapped out. In the figure below, this is represented by the initial broad idea that leads you to the literature and other source materials, where you will refine your idea into a study question.

Iterative Process in Producing the Project Plan

Broad
Idea

Body of
Literature
and Source
Materials

Project
Structure or
Design

Study
Question

Specific Aims and
Complete Project Plan

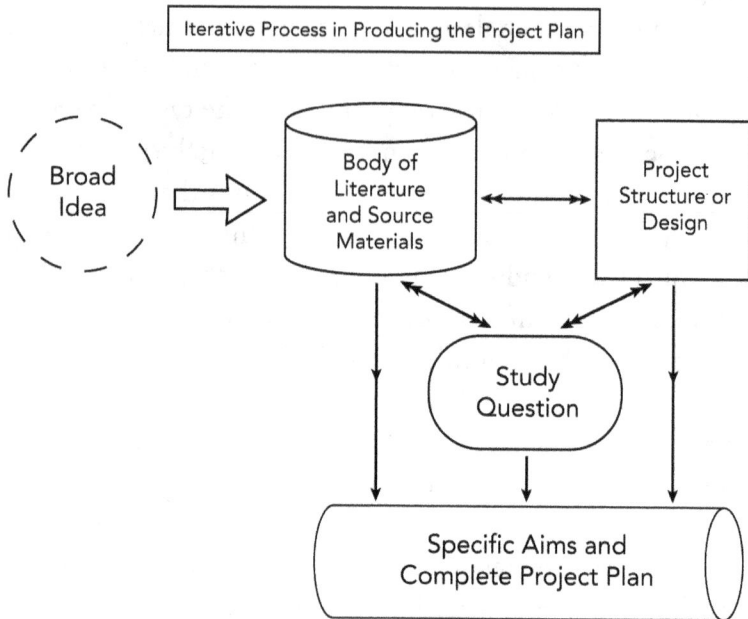

Refining the study question requires intellectual integration of the information in the literature with the design or structure of your study, and reviews of your study question through that integrated lens. Once the study question is final, it drives the decision about study design and narrows the field of published research that you will address in your plan.

These are the three fundamental components of a research project plan: the literature, the project structure, and the study question. All three come together as a whole and complete plan of action.

Non-Experimental Research Designs

Let's take a look at four non-e project designs. The design or structure you select will depend on your study question.

If you already have an idea for your project, consider how it would apply in each of these designs as you read through the material. Just read, though—don't try to memorize or apply them to your project. Just get familiar with them.

Non-e designs are for studies that do not use an intervention or treatment. Variables are not manipulated. The data may be new or existing.

Research Designs

Case-Control

Cohort

Cross-Sectional

Correlational

A topic or question that, for a variety of reasons, cannot be studied experimentally might be suitable for a non-experimental design.

Non-e designs are suited to exploration of conditions to learn more about them, develop theories, or analyze data from a new perspective. Non-e research can generate additional questions for study, or protocols that others may test. Findings from these designs may be published the same way as experimental research results.

You may hear and see a lot of different names for research designs that do not involve experimentation. Always ask the person to tell you more about the design or structure they are using. For example, someone says "this is a descriptive study." That's a relatively easy one. They probably already have data they will use to narrate observations. However, "a descriptive study" is not actually a "design." It is a project approach or structure. It is what you do with the data you collect.

Another consideration is that all of the designs I cover could be referred to as descriptive studies using a "specified" design.

When you select a non-e design, it's best to adhere to the traditional terminology. You will be clear, and others with whom you discuss your project will be clear about what you are going to do to address the study question.

Each design calls for specific data to be collected and specific statistical tests to be applied.

Although you will encounter differences in the labels applied to some designs depending on the professional field of study, the ones I provide here are the most common types of non-experimental research designs. Each design can be associated with a specifically worded study aim or question. Each one has a specific shape and purpose, as well as limitations, strengths, and cautions.

In your profession, there are available textbooks and papers about research designs. You will find selected texts, papers, and websites listed in *Appendix 2. References and Resources,* where you can get more or different perspectives on these designs. Reading the literature in your field, noting the various designs used for different studies, will give you the applied perspective on these designs.

In the section below, I have provided brief descriptions only. *Appendix 1. Terminology, Study Designs & Project Structures* contains more detail about each study design, including examples and cautions.

Some designs may be combined to respond to the study question or the purpose of the study. You need to have your study question or aim clearly defined before selecting a study design or structure. You also need to have a good sense of the time and resources you will need to select the most suitable design.

All these designs begin with the letter C.
Try not to get confused.
Each design is associated with a specific type of primary study question and a number of groups.

Case-Control Design

Two Groups: Matched on specified characteristics. Usually retrospective, beginning with a condition or outcome, and working backward. Do subjects in the "case" group, all of whom have the condition of interest, differ on selected factors from subjects in the "control" group who do not have that condition?

A case-control design is used when you want to explain why some people develop or experience a certain condition while others do not.

This is the least likely design candidate for a student or trainee to use. Why?

First, there are two prescribed groups in this design. The groups must be matched on key characteristics. Second, you need access to data for both groups of people, one with and one without a specific condition of interest.

The purpose is to learn whether people with condition X differ in the exposure they have to risk factors from people without condition X. The condition can be a disease, or it might be a quality, a status, or a health outcome.

Strictly speaking, this design is used to create a prediction model for who will and who won't likely get a disease or illness. Use this design to determine how a condition is acquired or why it developed in some and not in others. The type of information gained from case-control studies informs early identification of persons at risk for condition X.

Typically, this design is used to gain insights into rare or little-understood conditions. These insights can provide valuable information for public health, treatment protocols, prevention strategies, and environmental concerns.

Public health and medical researchers often use this design, and it also lends itself to research in psychology, social work, and education. An example of a question suited to this design is: Do nulliparous women with post-partum depression have different perinatal exposures compared to a matched group of nulliparous women without post-partum depression?

How does this design work?

A case-control study determines, through the use of statistics called "odds ratios" and "confidence intervals," whether persons with the condition were at greater risk (i.e., had more exposure/factors) than those who did not develop the condition.

Groups must be matched to protect against bias or errors.

Before selecting this design, or creating a question that would require this design, consult a biostatistician on the sample size needed to calculate odds ratios. Also consult an expert on the condition in which you are interested.

If you cannot obtain sufficient cases to satisfy your desired precision, there are several steps you can take.

a. You can reconsider the value of the study topic relative to the effort required or to its overall value to the field.

b. You can consider modifying your definitions to narrow the focus.

c. You can craft a question that would be related to your interest but suited to a simpler design.

d. You could, with your advisor's approval, proceed with fewer cases than a power analysis indicates are needed for study integrity but sufficient enough to use statistical analysis tools, acknowledging that the study has limitations.

Cohort Study Design

One Group: Measurements taken over time to examine change.

A cohort study design allows the researcher to examine changes in an observation of interest from one point to another, within one group. The key in this design is measuring change.

This is the second least likely design candidate for a student or trainee to use. Why?

First, although a cohort study is exploratory and developmental and may lead to larger research and theory building, it can very easily become large and unfeasible within time constraints.

Because you would follow subjects over time, prospectively or retrospectively, there is a risk of losing study subjects. Thus, you need a larger than necessary number of enrolled subjects or available cases to account for attrition.

Further, it can be analytically demanding because the questions most suited for it would be aimed at establishing thresholds and goals for treatment interventions as well as health or learning outcomes.

How does the design work?

The researcher measures a variable of interest at a defined baseline and again at a defined endpoint. Usually, the study begins at the baseline time point and ends at the point defined as the end of the study time period. However, the design may be used to look at a group in the past as well.

A cohort design should be considered in a study aimed at providing insight to factors that contribute to the outcome and possibly improving intervention strategies.

Here are three examples.

- A clinic started using cognitive behavioral therapy (CBT) a year earlier, where you could access a sample of female patients between the ages of 25 and 35, with specific diagnoses, to examine changes in existing pre and post-CBT testing scores.
- Measure students' attitudes toward online learning at the beginning of a school year and again at the end of a semester or the school year.
- Using existing data, you could compare the average income in multiple cities in one census year to the average income in the next census year.

Your question is not about whether certain conditions contributed to an outcome, only whether there are changes between the first measurement and the last measurement. For prospective studies, there is a risk of losing study subjects. Changes might be explained by various conditions or events along the way.

Cross-Sectional Design

One or More Groups: A single point in time, to estimate prevalence or compare change.
Cross-sectional means the sample is drawn at a specific point in time from one population.
This is a good option for student research projects, with certain precautions.

First, you must have sufficient number of cases to estimate prevalence in one group.

Second, if you include a comparison group, you must match the groups, and measure a condition at a specific time point for all groups.

This type of design can be used for research questions that are not driven by a hypothesis but are focused on a little-understood phenomenon. A cross-sectional design is suitable for estimating prevalence of a condition in a population, generating questions for future research, or possibly improving our understanding of the prevalence of a condition. With an adequate number of cases, this design can be used to richly describe a population, using exploratory data analysis tools.

Correlational Design

One Group: Sampling is not time-sensitive. Suited for existing data. Are selected variables related to each other in that group?

This is the simplest design for a student project. Why?

A correlational design is used to examine or explore relationships between selected characteristics, qualities, or conditions within one group.

The word correlational means variables influence each other.

An example is income increasing as age increases.

Variables may be co-related positively or negatively. As one changes the other changes.

You could use continuous data to ask whether final exam scores are related to hours of sleep. You can use nominal variables, such as gender or race, to determine the extent to which they are related to color preference.

One nice feature of correlational studies is that you can use existing data without sampling. If your mentor has a large data set from an experimental research study, you might be permitted to explore a subset of those data.

Use this design if you think a variable is different depending on the properties of another variable.

Here are four examples.

- In a group of graduates from nursing school, income increased as they grew older.
- Does age affect recovery time from knee injuries?
- Are different professions related to quality-of-life measures?
- Are case dispositions in a juvenile justice center related to the type of charges (violent/nonviolent) or previous incarcerations?

With this design for a project, you can study two variables or use a more complex factorial design with multiple variables. In this study design, the statistical tests look for direction and strength of relationships between variables. Correlation results help generate questions for future research, generate theories, or develop models for testing. This design is relatively easy to manage.

Analyses of these data are intriguing because you can use visual graphics such as scatter plots to look at the shape of the data. One useful example is The Circumplex Model of Marital and Family Systems (CMMFS; Olson, Sprenkle, & Russell, 1979), in which both linear and curvilinear relationships can be found.

Other Research Project Structures

These project structures are not traditionally referred to as "designs." That is not as important as whether your study question is best suited for one of these approaches.

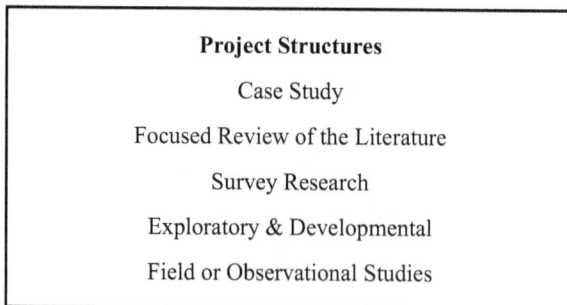

Project Structures

Case Study

Focused Review of the Literature

Survey Research

Exploratory & Developmental

Field or Observational Studies

Case Study

One individual or multiple cases of a rare condition or observation. Not a sample.

A case study is not a *case control* study. This type of project structure is used to gain a more in-depth understanding of a rare or complex phenomenon.

A case study requires the use of analytic and critical thinking skills to decipher sequences and recognize patterns. It requires extensive knowledge of other conditions to put a case in context. It can also be used to describe a new procedure or a complex diagnosis. You could consider a case study to explore challenges in diagnostic processes.

A case study project can use more than one case with the same condition or phenomenon. It may be feasible to extrapolate, or pull and pool, information and data or statistics from several case studies to make observations that might yield insights otherwise not revealed in one case study. Be creative!

Health professions students have ample opportunities to observe rare or complex cases and analyze several with analytic narratives under a phenomenological umbrella. For example, nursing students may be interested in describing cases of teenage patients who do and don't recover from intensive care following car accidents in which they were driving. Physicians' Assistant students might observe health status anomalies in primary care patients over age 65. Social work students might be interested in personal care challenges of medically fragile pre-school children.

It is the story told by the case details that contribute to our understanding of recovery in this situation.

Each professional group has websites and literature that would guide you in a feasible and meaningful direction if you choose this strategy. A case study is an excellent opportunity to incorporate interdisciplinary or interprofessional aspects of healthcare delivery.

Focused Review of the Literature

A focused review of the literature in your topic of interest is not a study design, per se, but it is an approach suitable for a scholarly project. The purpose of a focused review is to determine the extent of the evidence-base for creating, modifying, clarifying, or simply considering alternatives to current practice. This is not a meta-analysis, so you would not use data or statistical tests. You would not be concerned about the validity of your study.

Survey Research

This is not technically a study design, but it is sometimes thought of that way. A survey is really a research tool: a method of collecting information. You can use a survey with a cross-sectional study design, taking a survey at one point in time with one group. You might see this term used as if it were a study design. If you choose to do or develop and test a survey as a project, think of it as a correlational study.

Exploratory & Developmental

If you do not have a specific study question, but you have a study aim, you might consider this approach to the project. This is not a traditional design for testing a hypothesis or a study question. In an exploratory and developmental study, the question would be broad for a topic that has not been well researched.

You've heard of this type of research referred to as a fishing expedition, as in throw out that line and see what you catch. In statistics, this is discouraged because of the assumptions underlying statistical tests. Nevertheless, if the purpose of your study is to explore relationships among variables in a large data set because it is large and unexamined, this might be the approach to use.

Suppose you want to develop a new questionnaire to define attitudes toward poverty. This would be the approach preferable to a cross-sectional or correlational design because you aren't studying a population as much as you are using their information to create an instrument that could be used in other populations to detect the presence or absence of perspectives you are studying.

If you want to better understand what a population looks like or what qualities characterize leadership styles among department heads in different professions, you could use a cross-sectional or correlational study design with the purpose of exploring the variables of interest.

For exploring meaning in a large data set, or the shape of data in a large group, you can use this approach with a cross-sectional sample. Again, if you have a specific quantified question, go for a more traditional design.

Field or Observational Studies

Observational studies draw inferences from a sample population to the relevant general population. These types of studies are usually in vivo. In real life, the researcher goes into a community or location and collects information through observation. A quintessential example of this approach is Jane Goodall's research among wild chimpanzees. (*https://www.janegoodall.org/*)

Case studies, cross-sectional studies, and cohort study designs may incorporate observation as a method for collecting data. This type of study is meant for real world information gathering, collecting observations of people or animals in natural or contrived conditions that are not experimental. In healthcare research, guidelines may be applicable to meet criteria that guards against errors in this type of research.

Feasibility and Planning Strategies (Template 1)

Now let's turn our attention to what makes a project feasible and how to plan within your available time and resources.

Unfeasible plans lead to dissatisfaction. To maintain your balance and momentum, your project needs to be realistic and "doable" in the real world. The principles of feasibility apply to the purpose, intent, scope, and logistics of any project. For any research study, no matter how small or large, each stage and each action step must be carefully developed, defined, and communicated throughout the plan.

At the beginning, you need to think about *project goals, milestones, and deadlines.* Create a schedule of regular, agenda-driven meetings with key individuals, advisors, and other experts. Don't skip a meeting because you think there is nothing to discuss. You might miss out on an important opportunity.

Template 1. Project Feasibility Checklist guides you through a set of questions to decide whether and how your project can be completed with the time, resources, and tasks you must accomplish. It contains a schedule you can complete with goals and expectations explicitly defined. It will help you be prepared to enter the planning phase with confidence.

Although there is no magic formula to determine if a project is feasible, and anything can happen, this template will help you to anticipate and evaluate factors that can make your journey easier and help you to avoid unforeseen obstacles to completion. Attending to them early can save you time and improve the likelihood of success.

The best use of the template would be to type or write in your response to each item by yourself first, and then review them with your advisor. Together you may think of other questions that are important to answer before finalizing your project aim or research question and beginning your project.

Project feasibility should be considered from the moment you have a research project idea, throughout the process of finalizing your study question or aims. You should revisit the question of feasibility all along the path.

Key points to consider to ensure project feasibility

▶ The credibility and relevance of the sources of your idea
▶ The potential value of your study to the field
▶ The study design you want to use
▶ Having an advisor in your field, a biostatistician, and other content or process experts, such as people who work where the data reside
▶ Your own skills and knowledge
▶ Availability of tangible and intangible resources, including data collection tools, computer for data entry, software for analysis, forms, applications, protocols, transportation, permissions, and approvals
▶ Sufficient time to complete the project given its scope and size
▶ The goals, milestones and schedules, and expectations, your own and those of others

Skills and Abilities Essential for a Successful Research Project (Template 2)

Before you begin tackling the work of developing your project and creating the plan, it will help you to have twenty core skills and abilities for planning and conducting research.

Sometimes we overlook the obvious. In this case the obvious would be if you can't organize materials, or sift through and discard nonessential information, or define your study variables, you may not be ready to develop a research project plan, and surely not ready to conduct research.

These twenty skills and abilities are the platform from which you can confidently proceed to create a feasible, elegant project plan. I've created a checklist for you to use in determining whether you already have, or need to acquire, these core skills and abilities.

Use this list to ask yourself if you have, or if you need to acquire, each skill set. If you see any skill that you need to develop, ask for help on how to acquire that skill, and then practice.

You can use this list to discuss the various skills and abilities with your advisor prior to beginning your planning document. This list is also available in Template 2. Skills and Abilities Checklist. That template provides a checklist you can complete and track your acquisition of skills and abilities, a rating scale to track your level of confidence in each skill, and a guide to deciding how to acquire each skill.

Use that template to make notes on how you plan to acquire any skills and abilities you may need before beginning a research project. Use it to review your skill set with your advisors.

List of Essential Core Skills and Abilities

- Knowledge of the topic of interest
- Interest, curiosity about a specific observed phenomenon
- Organization of thoughts (e.g., goal orientation, thinking skills, problem solving)
- Analytic thinking**
- Critical thinking**
- Time Management (Scheduling, Planning)
- Writing (Grammar, Structure, Logic)
- General Vocabulary (comprehension)
- Research Vocabulary (comprehension)
- Patience (calm when obstacles arise, allowances for delays)
- Diligence (careful, persistent, thorough)
- Scanning a literature database efficiently
- Excluding nonessential information to narrow the focus
- Basic conversational knowledge of statistics
- Human Subjects Protection principles and practices
- Ethical (Honesty, Forthright, Judicious, Discrete, Fair)
- Organization of tasks (space, transportation, resource acquisition)
- Communication (Clarity of thought, verbal specificity)
- Flexibility (Able to adjust to challenges, Creative – "outside the box" approaches to obstacles)
- Integrity (Respectful, Truthful, Open minded)

**Analytic thinking and critical thinking are sometimes confused. They are different mental activities with different purposes and outcomes.

Analytic thinking can be thought of as the mental act of breaking down complex information, data, or facts into smaller parts for the purpose of organizing them and applying logic and reasoning to achieve a greater understanding of patterns, relationships, or other revelations. No judgement is involved. Activities involved in analytic thinking include:

1. Examining chunks of facts, data, or information and eliminating extraneous elements.
2. Applying logic to organize and sort information into meaningful sub-sets.
3. Identifying patterns or trends and considering relationships among the sub-sets.
4. Making observations.

Critical thinking involves mental activities engaging the right brain to evaluate information and interpret it using insight, perspective, context, and judgement. Analytic thinking is, however, an essential first step in the process of critical thinking. Activities involved in critical thinking include:

1. Collecting information, data, and facts about a clearly stated problem or issue.
2. Evaluating the credibility and accuracy of those data.
3. Applying analysis tools to understand the context, precipitating factors, or reasons for the stated problem.
4. Creatively analyzing information for a deeper understanding of a situation, or to generate researchable questions or theories, and formulate strategies to address the problem.

THREE

The Research Project Plan – A Macro View

Overview

This chapter provides an orientation to the four major sections of a Research Project Plan (RPP). It begins with the outline. You will become familiar with the nature and purpose of each section before diving into writing them. Later in the book, you will understand how the sections are interrelated to form a whole project plan. Your RPP may serve initially as the proposal, thus it serves two purposes. Upon approval, you have your roadmap for the journey.

Objectives of a research project plan

The RPP has two primary objectives. These objectives serve the researcher and an audience of advisors and consumers.

Objective 1: Describe the purpose, intent, scope, and importance of the project.

Objective 2: Establish protocols and procedures for conducting and completing the project in accordance with applicable rules and regulations.

The content of an RPP is not the same as a grant application. In fact, once funded, researchers often translate their grant proposals into logistical operations manuals to guide the project activities. That process typically involves defining and describing activities in more detail, linking milestones to goals in the form of schedules and checklists, and compiling lists of resources or actual measurement instruments. Of course, it is possible that your RPP may serve as a proposal until you have all necessary approvals to move forward.

In most academic settings, a research project plan is a public document that communicates to a specific audience that

✓ The researcher has a measurable question or aim that merits investigation.

✓ The activities required to address the question or achieve the aim can be accomplished and have all the necessary approvals and authorizations.

The RPP is a roadmap, a plan of action that guides your journey from a question to a discovery. It represents your personal connection to, and your investment in, the project.

In less than six pages, your plan describes the purpose, the question, the background, and rationale for your project, as well as all the steps and schedules for data collection and management, how you will analyze the data, and how you will interpret and report your findings. Your RPP will communicate to others the theoretical and professional practice frameworks of your study. It contains the following information.

> The aim and value of the project,
> What you will do,
> Why you will do it,
> How you will do it,
> When you will do it, and
> Under what conditions you will work.

A small-to-medium sized, non-experimental research or scholarly project plan should be about 4½ pages in length, with ½ page remaining for citations. In complex or longitudinal studies, it may approach six pages of narrative and tables, charts, or graphs, and one page for references. Follow local guidelines if they restrict the length.

There are multiple sources of guidance on the content and format of each section of a research plan in published textbooks, on academic websites, and on proprietary websites that require a subscription or membership. If you consult them, keep in mind that research project development, planning, and execution are not solitary processes. Writing a research plan is fundamentally the responsibility of one person, but you can benefit from the input of a team, consultant, advisor, and reviewer.

Essential sections in a research project plan

This book covers four core sections of a research project plan: Specific Aims, Background & Importance, Structure & Methods, and Human Subjects Protection.

Project Plan Sections – ideal number of pages

Specific Aims – ½ page

Background & Importance – 1 page

Structure & Methods – 2 pages

Human Subjects Protection – ½ **page**

Other sections depend on the type of project you are planning and may include Budget, Resources, Assurances, or the Environment.

If there are no specific formats preferred or required by your course or institution, this outline will work for you. If there are specific requirements, the material you create using this guide and the templates can be used to populate a different outline. Always check the requirements for the intended recipient agent.

Research projects involving human subjects' data must be approved by the authority governing human subjects' research at your institution or sponsoring organization before you begin any part of the project. Some projects need more than one set of approvals or authorizations.

Be sure you comply with your local policies and rules.

Specific Aims

This is the plan overview. It's an executive summary of the project. It is like the ingredients for a cake recipe in narrative form. The rest of the plan contains the instructions to mix, bake, decorate, and present the final product. You will write this section last.

What's the point?

In less than ½ of a page, the reader has access to the essential elements of your project. It brings together all the other parts of the project plan in one paragraph.

This section of the RPP contains five elements.

1. A high-impact introduction to the topic.
2. The primary study question or aim, and possibly its corollary null hypothesis.
3. A high-level statement of why you want to conduct this study and the value or contribution it will make to the field.
4. A summary of the structure & methods.
5. A convincing punch line.

Example of Specific Aims Content

> *A high-impact introduction to the topic.*

From the literature search, you confirm that self-esteem is related to a history of childhood trauma, a contributing risk factor for major depressive disorder (MDD). The cost to the healthcare system and to society is high. Use high-impact facts to illustrate this and underscore the topic's importance.

> *The primary research question and a study hypothesis*

The research question is: *Are low self-esteem and a history of childhood trauma associated with recovery from depression in young adult women?* My null hypothesis is logically, *Recovery from depression does not depend on self-esteem or a history of childhood trauma.* Alternatively, a study aim might be *the purpose of this study is to increase our understanding of factors contributing to or impeding recovery from depression, specifically whether self-esteem and childhood trauma mitigate MDD remission.*

> *A high-level statement of why you should study this question and its broader implications for the field.*

The reason you believe you should study this topic is to discover treatment or screening implications for depression in young women. The literature suggests the current screening tools might be missing true positive cases and do not include questions on self-esteem. It also notes that true positives are more often missed in women of color. You can use a correlational design. This project aims *to add to our current understanding of the extent to which self-esteem and childhood trauma are related to MDD symptom remission.*

> *Summary of the structure & methods for the study.*

In a few short sentences, tell the reader: a) the design/approach, b) what is the study population, c) what variables you are measuring and how they are defined, d) what data you will collect, where it is, and how you will collect it, e) the approach to the analysis and statistical tests you will use for the primary and secondary questions.

> *A convincing punch line.*

The punch line pulls it all together to confidently declare the project's intrinsic and extrinsic value, that it is clearly defined, and has a specific goal or aim that can be achieved.

Example: If low self-esteem is associated with a history of childhood trauma, and childhood trauma is a factor in developing depressive symptoms, clinical evaluations should consider including self-esteem as a potential obstacle to symptom remission in young women, with possible additional focus on women of color.

The statement may not make you cry, or fall on your knees, but it shouldn't prompt a self-inflicted forehead slap either. It can be bold, or modest, as long as it summarizes your overall goal of contributing to our understanding of the topic.

The Specific Aims section is the executive summary. It appears first, but you will write it last, after the Background & Importance and the Structure & Methods sections are final. Strive to keep the Specific Aims section to ½ page or less; about 250 – 300 words. This count is for Times New Roman, 12pt font, single-spaced lines. You will provide all the details in the next two sections of the plan.

Background & Importance

What's the point?

The background is the context of your project, the platform upon which it rests. It provides information to illustrate that the study is important and grounded in credible information and adjunctive to current knowledge.

This section of the plan situates your project relative to the research that has already been done and the findings that inspired your study question or aim. It answers the question, "how does my study fit into the landscape of published information on the topic?"

Background refers to the history and context of what we know about the topic and question your project addresses.

Importance refers to the value or benefit of your study.

Background sets the stage; importance is the impact of the activities that occur on that stage. Background and importance are interdependent.

This is the section of the plan where you distill and discuss scientific knowledge of the topic, link it to your study question, and logically narrate how your study adds value to the existing knowledge. Your narrative summarizes available and relevant scientific knowledge on the subject and justifies its further investigation.

In this section, you will summarize the conclusions of previous studies as well as the questions generated by those studies that remain unanswered. For a manuscript or a grant proposal, there would be more information than what you need in a project plan. A project plan includes only essential information about what we know and do not know, or need to better understand about the topic, and how your study will fill or bridge those gaps and increase knowledge in the field.

You will use this material later when you report your findings.

The Background & Importance section addresses these five questions.

1. What are the latest, most important, and relevant facts on the study topic, and its question or aim?
2. What do published research findings, most closely related to your question, tell us about this topic or question?
3. What aspects of this area need further understanding or exploration?
4. What is the benefit to seeking additional knowledge in this area?
5. How do items 1 through 3 provide a rationale for your study aims?

Chapter Six provides instructions for constructing this section of the plan, with these five questions expanded to ten-point outline.

Structure & Methods

What's the point?

Structure refers to the study design or approach you will use to address the question or study aim/goal. Methods include the tasks necessary to address the question or test the hypothesis.

This section may also be called "Research Design & Methods." It contains the practical information about the organization of the project and describes all the tools and tasks needed to complete it.

If you were to investigate the NIH guidelines for grant applications, you would see that it currently uses the term "Research Strategy" for this section, calling for a distinctive narrative according to the nature of the project. However, a grant proposal still must contain information about the study design, and how the researcher will collect, manage, and analyze data.

Regardless of the title used for this section of an RPP, the same elements must be included. I've used the term "Structure & Methods" to place front and center, in your mind, the two main parts of this narrative. I use this term also, because guidelines in most professional and research journals, and scholarly academic products continue to use the terms "design and methods" for the research report. The word "structure" allows for greater flexibility in the study project approach.

This section calls for considerable specificity in how the researcher will examine or test the data associated with each study aim or question. It allows for a broader perspective than a restrictive and technical narration of a scientific "research design" because not all studies use a specific research design in the technical sense of the word.

The Structure & Methods section covers every detail about how your project is organized, and why that design or approach is suitable for answering the study question or achieving the study aims. In this section, you will also describe the statistical methods you will use for testing the primary question, how you will collect and manage data, and all activities necessary to conduct and complete the project.

This section requires about two to three pages of material. You can use the writing tips in Chapter Twelve to help you find your voice, cover enough details to gain approval for your project, and to conduct it in compliance with relevant rules or regulations.

If the local requirements permit, you can use flow charts as a tool to save space and clearly illustrate the sequencing of tasks. A flow chart can make a complex process easier to follow than discussing it in a narrative.

A thorough Structure & Methods narrative should contain enough details for another person to replicate the project or to locate additional information about the study methods. The guiding principle for writing this section is to provide evidence that the plan you have to conduct and complete the project meets the following expectations.

✓ Appropriately structured and organized to address the question
✓ Logically developed
✓ Seamlessly managed
✓ Reasonably able to be done with available resources

To achieve this, you will address these six points.

1. The study design or project structure you are using and how it suits your study question
2. Statistical power of the study
3. Study population and sampling method
4. Data collection and management
5. Analysis strategies and tests
6. Timelines, with backup plans for anticipated problems

Instructions and templates to construct this section are in Chapter Seven.

Human Subjects

What's the point?

This section describes all the elements of your study that relate to individuals who participate or whose information you use.

In human history, peoples have been irreparably harmed by unregulated research. In the United States, federal laws govern the rights, well-being, and welfare of humans involved in research. State and local organizations must comply with these laws. The Office for Human Research Protections (OHRP) at the Health and Human Services agency provides a compilation of rules in 133 countries and classifies them into categories of application. You can find them currently at

https://www.hhs.gov/ohrp/international/compilation-human-research-standards/index.html.

All states have offices that issue policies on human research protections. The NIH has a "decision tool" that you can complete for guidance on steps you must take for your type of research to ensure that study participants and their information are protected. If you answer the questions precisely, the tool will tell you if you meet exempt or non-exempt criteria. From there, you can proceed to contact your local OHRP or personnel who support the Institutional Review Board activities.

Today, anyone who conducts research in the United States must be certified. The program of today is called CITI. That is the Collaborative Institutional Training Initiative. It ensures that all institutions governing human research have consistent training for their researchers. *https://about.citiprogram.org/en/homepage/*

FOUR

The Study Question

Overview

This chapter will walk you through the process of developing a measurable study question. It also addresses the alternative strategy of using a study or project aim or goal. Aim is a more specific term, as it suggests a clear target, so that is the term I will use. The process isn't much different because whether you have a question or an aim, both must be measurable, or able to be addressed scientifically with precise analyses.

There are many steps and stages in the formation of a study question. You start with an idea, make speculations about it, narrow the focus, and create a question for which you can reasonably obtain quantitative and/or qualitative data that can be analyzed to yield a result, and answer, or a set of findings.

What is a question?

A question is a statement formulated in a way that calls for information that you need to acquire insight into a condition or event, leading to an answer or decision.

Here's a bit oversimplified example of the path along which one might travel to formulate a measurable question about what to have for dinner.

Example: The Dinner Decision

Measurable question: What would <u>taste good</u> for dinner that would be <u>healthy</u>?
Criteria: Tasty and healthy.
Refine the question: Define healthy.
Define healthy: Food that contains nutrients: fish, chicken, vegetables
Define tasty: Flavorful, enjoy eating it
More information about variables: Fish is too expensive. Vegetables can be a side dish (secondary question as to what type)
Select variable of interest: Chicken.
Define chicken: There are different characteristics and qualities of chicken that I should consider.
Construct the approach to answer the question:
Measures of chicken: Nutrition qualities, safety qualities, cooking methods
Definitions of the measures: Skinless, amount of antibiotics, recipes
Type of data for each measure: nominal, continuous, ordinal, interval, ratio?
Classifying measures and data: How will I organize the data according to the rating scales needed? For example, to rate how much antibiotic in chicken is harmful. How will I define harmful?

Collect all the data, determine the least harmful, most tasty pieces of chicken, and make your decision.

You might have several different chicken dinners and rate how you feel after each one.

You could invite friends to eat with you and ask them to rate the chicken dishes (taste, fat content, eye appeal, fragrance, and such).

Eventually, your mind works like a computer on day-to-day "research questions." You acquire information, evaluate and measure it, analyze it, and draw conclusions.

What is involved in developing my study question?

The first step in creating a viable framework for a research project is formulating the study question. Your project might have an aim, or a goal, but it begins, as any journey, with one important question, a question that beckons and engages your curiosity.

In the following material, I'll walk you through the process of formulating that important question and how to make it measurable.

The mind usually works from the macro level to the micro level; that is, from broad ideas or observations to a narrower focus with more specificity. Extrapolation and inductive reasoning work in the opposite direction.

While a small percent of people notices detail first and then fill out the edges to construct the whole picture, it is more likely that you will make a general observation, speak to the big picture, with curiosity about its nature or meaning, and then attend to details. For that reason, you will probably not begin this journey with a specific measurable question.

Where should my question come from?

In your studies, you have learned to examine information, question it, and practice what you learn. Research project opportunities are everywhere. Questions should be just popping out of your coursework: Why does this information contradict that information? What trends have produced X effect? What don't we know about a subject? Have I gotten answers to questions in classes or at a presentation that satisfied my curiosity?

Maybe you have seen a patient or a client with a set of conditions similar to another patient but with different diagnoses, and the individuals were from different racial or ethnic backgrounds. And later, you attend a grand rounds presentation or journal club about psychiatric diagnoses and race. Maybe then you begin to wonder if there are differences in diagnostic profiles between races.

You may have a number of fleeting thoughts, but if you want a meaningful project, write them down or record them to consider later. Carry 3x5 index cards with you to write your ideas. Send yourself a text or record a note on your phone. Is that nerdy? Well, maybe. Smart? Definitely.

Reading the literature on your topic will inform you about various study designs and data analysis others have used for the topic of your interest. You can formulate your own question for a local exploratory study. In fact, you could base your entire project on one premise or one question from one published article as long as you have supporting evidence that the question has not been answered and is an important one to advance knowledge in the field.

Let's consider some examples of inspiration for research project questions.

1. We hear alarms about physician shortages, yet the Institute of Medicine argues this shortage does not exist, suggesting that the system is inefficient and advanced practice providers, who are increasing in numbers, are insufficiently deployed. Availability of care has expanded with telemedicine platforms.

What questions come to mind in this area of policy and access to care? Here are three examples.

   a. If the average time primary care physicians spend with patients decreases, does that equate to poor quality care?
   b. How do counties in one state compare to counties in another state on health professional shortage area scores?
   c. Are laws governing the scope of practice for nurse practitioners and physician assistants related to the status of the health professional shortage area score?

2. Healthcare economics is an important realm to consider. Here are some facts. Around $3.6 trillion were spent in 2018 on healthcare in the United States. Healthcare spending is approaching 20% of the gross domestic product in this country. Hospitals and insurance companies account for a large portion of the cost of healthcare in this country. Employer-based health insurance covers more than 58% of the non-elderly population, but the premiums have risen, and the co-pay requirements increased. Economic, social, and other factors are barriers to access to care.

What questions come to mind in this topic? Here are two examples.

  a. What diseases are prevalent among low socioeconomic groups that increase the cost of indigent care because of limited access to healthcare?
  b. Is socioeconomic status related to satisfaction with healthcare in persons over 65, or in specified racial or ethnic populations?

3. Disease burden and poverty is another broad topic to explore. The U.S. may have the highest chronic disease burden, including approximately four-million people with a disability living in poverty. We know that the definition of poverty in the U.S. is manipulated at the federal government level to modify the criteria and manage the number of people who qualify for various programs. Nonetheless, almost one in every six children (nearly twelve million) lives in poverty, almost half of them in extreme poverty. Another almost two million children live in households hovering barely above the poverty line. Poverty is disproportionately distributed by race and ethnicity, as is access to healthcare and disease burden.

What questions come to mind in this topic? Here are two examples.

  a. What health disparities affect children under the age of five living in poverty?
  b. What health status factors are associated with executive function or impulsivity problems among children living in poverty in the U.S.?

4. In the U.S. in 2018, over fourteen million households experienced food insecurity. Infant mortality rates are poorly understood in

the U.S., and maternal health and safety concerns continue to place women and children at risk.

What questions come to mind on this topic? Here are two examples.

a. What are the trends in public school systems in the prevalence of food insecurity for children under age ten?

b. Do children of different racial and ethnic backgrounds experience different types or severities of food insecurities?

Research project ideas are everywhere. Keep in mind, though, that it isn't a research project if we already know the answer to the study question. If we only *partly* know the answer, then the field is ripe for investigating.

Base your project on the gaps in the literature or on the future directions recommended by the authors. Testable and measurable questions arise from challenging existing information or wondering if there is more information to fill a gap in available knowledge on a topic.

There are other processes useful for crafting a good study question. For example, mind mapping is a tool that many creative writers use. Here is an example of using mind mapping to connect a group of concepts and produce a question.

The central prompt in this sample mind map is the topic of *self-assessed health status.* The concepts that come to mind, plausibly related to health status, as assessed by the individual not by a clinician, include demographics, health conditions, socioeconomic status, and belief systems. A broad overall question might be: *What factors are associated with self-assessed health status?*

As we draw connecting lines between the variables, we think are related to the measure of self-assessed health status, we can begin to narrow the question to make it more focused and measurable.

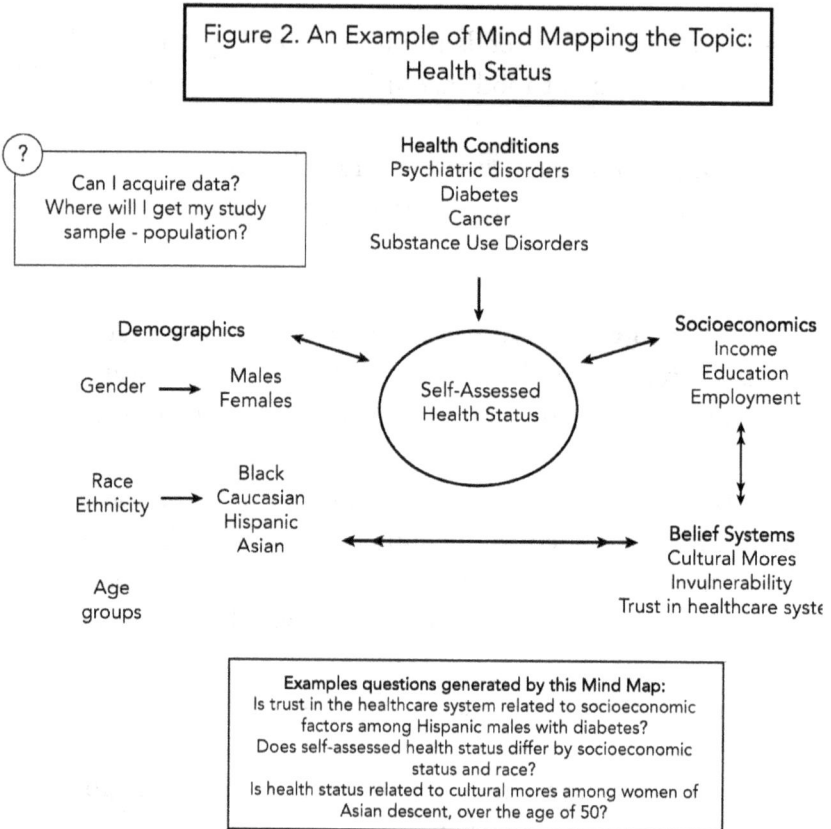

Figure 2. An Example of Mind Mapping the Topic: Health Status

? Can I acquire data? Where will I get my study sample - population?

Health Conditions
Psychiatric disorders
Diabetes
Cancer
Substance Use Disorders

Demographics

Gender ⟶ Males / Females

Race Ethnicity ⟶ Black / Caucasian / Hispanic / Asian

Age groups

Self-Assessed Health Status

Socioeconomics
Income
Education
Employment

Belief Systems
Cultural Mores
Invulnerability
Trust in healthcare syste

Examples questions generated by this Mind Map:
Is trust in the healthcare system related to socioeconomic factors among Hispanic males with diabetes?
Does self-assessed health status differ by socioeconomic status and race?
Is health status related to cultural mores among women of Asian descent, over the age of 50?

In the box, you see examples of questions that can be generated by this example mind map.

In addition to possible study questions, we have made another notation about whether data is available and accessible for a study of this topic. A question may need refining as you identify variables to quantify the concepts, but this is an excellent place to begin.

What makes a question "good"?

A good question is one concise statement about an observation that can be measured. *A question is able to be measured if it lends itself to using qualitative or quantitative data to find, develop, or reveal a meaningful answer.*

If you decide to use a project aim, rather than a question, such as "to describe," "to explore," or "to increase our understanding of," the second part of the aim is going to be the question phrased as a topic or condition.

Before you finalize your study question, make certain that you can measure it with available or obtainable information. Here are two examples of broad questions and aims that need more precision to be measurable.

Question 1: Are teenagers with executive functioning impairments more likely to be arrested or placed in a psychiatric treatment facility?

Aim 1: The purpose of this study is to better understand the role of executive functioning impairments in placing an adolescent at risk for incarceration versus commitment to treatment.

Question 2: What is difference in executive functioning between teens arrested and incarcerated, and teens detained and placed in a psychiatric facility?

Aim 2: The aim of this study is to describe executive functioning differences between incarcerated and inpatient treatment adolescents.

These two questions are broad. How can they be refined to become measurable?

You would work through the following three steps you need to take.

First, you must define executive functioning impairments. Executive functioning is comprised of several skills and abilities, including self-awareness, working memory, and problem solving. Not all teens will have documented neuropsychological test results for these skills and abilities. You might have to query the local juvenile justice center and psychiatric hospital/s to determine what data are available.

If the response is incomplete or inconsistent, you can consider a proxy for executive functioning such as ratings assigned by intake psychology staff, or seek permission to collect from each adolescent a short questionnaire that assesses perceived competencies. The idea of a proxy measurement must be carefully explored due potential to self-reporting biases.

Revised Question: Do self-reported executive functioning skills and abilities differ between teens in detention and teens in psychiatric inpatient treatment?

Second, although this question alone is all right, there are other factors you could consider to ensure the homogeneity of the population for accurate analysis, such as diagnoses, age, number of previous admissions and/or offenses, gender, school status, and a measure of self-esteem, or sense of personal responsibility.

Third, does the literature support this approach? You discover that it does. The question allows you to develop a correlational study using only one group because you have two or more measures of perceived skills and abilities and other psychological constructs that are related to behaviors in adolescents. You also have two gender groups, and you may be able to determine the violent/nonviolent nature of charges if you work with a juvenile justice population.

How do you develop a question that can be measured? (Template 3)

As you have seen in the example above, most initial questions are be too broad to reasonably measure. But you can narrow a question using analytical or critical thinking, according to the nature of the phenomenon you are studying.

HOW DO YOU DIVIDE 17 POTATOES BETWEEN 4 PEOPLE?

MASH 'EM.

www.CartoonStock.com

There are many ways we could break down the process of developing a measurable question that sets up a feasible project.

The process I've used in this book involves a cycle of mental processes leading to the final measurable question. These mental processes are: making an observation; speculating about the observation; formulating a question based on the speculation; and validating the question with a fact-checking exercise. This four-step mental activity is repeated one more time before considering data availability, which sheds light on project scope and size. With that information, the study question is reviewed, validated with another fact-checking exercise, and revised as needed before checking data availability a second time against the revised question. At that point, the data list should be shorter and easier to manage, and a final study question can be formulated.

Although this may appear daunting at first, each iteration will bring additional clarity and specificity to the study question or aim.

In the material below, you'll walk through each step in the process of formulating a measurable study question, using one example. We'll cover selection of variables and some essential statistical considerations, and review the purpose and value of meeting with a biostatistician early in the process. Finally you'll find one additional example of the question formulation process.

The topic for this exercise in formulating a measurable study question is children and reading comprehension.

1. Observe: Make a statement about your topic of interest.

Reports are that more children are finishing elementary school with deficient reading comprehension skills and abilities. Illiteracy rates overall are increasing among children in elementary school.

2. Speculate about what you observed, such as why it occurs, how it manifests, what it means.

You think that perhaps reading comprehension scores in your state's public school districts could be related to increasing class sizes, or resources for remediating reading deficiencies, or to poorer language skills and abilities at entry into grade school, and more resources focused on STEM courses. Statistically, you believe that schools in the bottom quartile might contribute to this rate increase.

3. Question: Pose one or more plausible initial research questions.

Are scores in reading comprehension associated with class sizes, student–teacher ratios, or availability of remediation interventions?

4. Validate: Return to the literature or other source material to check the accuracy, relevance, and truth or veracity of your speculation and subsequent question. Is it on target? Is there information that suggests we already have the answer?

The question, as it is currently constructed, is broad and multi-faceted. You do more research into the topic. Upon further investigation, you find no evidence that reading comprehension and class size are related. You discover that two out of three children nationwide did not meet reading proficiency standards last year, and that remediation models are experimental and beyond the reach of schools with high volumes of socioeconomically distressed children. However, you do find information about measures of reading comprehension skills and abilities for every elementary school in your state.

5. Observe with increased focus: Using the information you found from returning to source materials, revise or amend your observation.

Based on new information, you note that in three school districts in your state, the proportion of children with below average scores on the statewide reading comprehension test increased from 10% to 15% in the past five years. This seems important.

6. Speculate with increased focus: Make statements about the nature of the revised observation, incorporating new information into what you think about it.

Now you are thinking that higher rates of reading comprehension deficiency may be related to the socioeconomic status of children in a district, or to other demographics.

7. Question with increased focus: Reshape the initial question/s to narrow the topic, and be more specific about key facets of your speculation.

What classes, and which children, contributed to the increased rate of reading comprehension deficits in those three districts?

8. Validate to narrow the question: Using your revised question, investigate the literature and source materials to drill down to a smaller arena, or to exclude extraneous variables. What do you discover? How does new information affect your revised question or speculations?

This would be a large study. With additional reading, you discover that there may be important differences in reading comprehension scores between racial, ethnic, and socioeconomic groups. You find that fifth and sixth grades receive the most attention in studies of reading comprehension. You also learn that reading comprehension scores consist of three distinct elements, each of which might explain variations across demographics.

9. Consider data availability: If you cannot obtain data for the project as it is currently defined, you'll want to revise the question. If you can, you should consider the size and scope of the project that the current question sets up.

What data are available to you? You can obtain information on each of the three elements that comprise the overall reading comprehension scores for all sixth grade classes in all the school districts.

10. Question reformulation: Using previous information, the element in which you have the most interest, and data availability, revise or reformulate a study question, with even greater specificity.

Using previously gathered information, and keeping in mind the importance of limiting the scope and size of the project, you can now restructure the question.

Do scores on the three core measures of reading comprehension differ between sixth grade classes in schools by the socioeconomic status of the district?

11. Validate: Review your question once again, with consideration for its value and how your question is supported by published research in this topic.

This question sets up a large study, using all the school districts in your state. That is a lot of data! Also, you learn that you are unable to obtain socioeconomic data for each child, but you discover that you could use a proxy for that measure by ranking the school district based on the proportion of students qualifying for public aid programs. However, there are other variables that interest you and may explain differences better than a district's socioeconomic status.

12. Revise your question once again, as needed: Refine the question so that you can measure it, so the project is not so large as to be unfeasible, and the scope is narrow enough to be meaningful.

This may seem like a redundant step, but consider that every time you read your study question aloud, it has a rhythm, a message. Is it specific enough for the project to be feasible—not too broad in scope, and not too large in terms of data collection or task demands?

Do reading comprehension scores differ between sixth grade classes on the basis of race and ethnicity?

While this question **is measurable**, reconsider the questions of scope and size.

13. Consider data availability: Carefully consider what data you need and can collect, manage, store, and analyze.

Returning to earlier information about the range of scores among the school districts, upon inquiry, you learn that you can easily obtain individual student reading comprehension scores on each of the elements that comprise "reading comprehension" for the three lowest scoring school districts' sixth grade classes and for a control group at the highest scoring districts. Knowing this enables you to focus the question on only six school districts' sixth grade classes.

14. Finalize the question: With that consideration, you could rephrase the question.

Do reading comprehension scores differ among students by race and ethnicity, and between school districts according to the districts' socioeconomic status?

What are you proposing?

For this project, you propose to answer this question for six districts in X state. You could also include other factors in the analysis, such as student–teacher ratio data or grade point average.

As a bonus, you discover that local schools' reading comprehension scores have not been studied from a simply descriptive viewpoint of racial and ethnic groups. This adds value to your study.

Alternatively, you could use a study aim instead of a question. For example: *The aim of this study is to describe the children in six school districts in X state, three with the lowest and three with the highest reading comprehension scores in Q year.* With this aim, you will describe the socioeconomic status of the schools in rich detail and test for differences in scores between age, gender, racial, and ethnic groups as well as overall academic performance.

Variables, Measures, and Statistical Considerations

It's not too soon to think about the way you will define the variables for your study. You know that a variable is a construct of interest that has a measurable quality (i.e., a trait or characteristic).

After you have the question—which you can be certain will change over the course of preparing your research project plan—the next step goes to the question of feasibility.

Ask yourself these two questions.

1. Does the question include the population and the phenomenon of interest specifically enough to define the data needed to address it?

2. What pieces of data—what variables—are best suited to define or describe the phenomenon and the conditions you posit to affect it, influence it, or be related to it?

Identifying Study Variables

The process of identifying variables for your study involves several interrelated steps. We'll use pediatric asthma as the topic.

Let's assume you have several ideas about a study with pediatric asthma patients.

Select the study question

For a case-control study, the question might be: are exposures different between children with and without asthma?

You discover that this question has been answered in the literature, but that there are a number of other areas of interest related to asthma in children that need to be studied. One example is that hospitals are paying close attention to preventing unnecessary use of emergency department services with strategies to prevent exacerbation of symptoms such as post-discharge care plans, care coordination team services, and routine wellness checks.

Based on that information, we might construct a study comparing two defined subgroups of this population on exposure to risks for asthma-related emergency department visits.

One subgroup might be patients who have a care coordination team assignment. The question here becomes: do asthma patients with a care coordination team use the ED less frequently than those without a care coordination team assignment? You select a correlational study design with two groups.

You are interested in whether children (age specific) who have a care coordination team assigned (usually post-discharge from a hospital stay) have better outcomes (defined) than a group with no care coordination team. This does not mean that you are investigating whether not having a care coordination team causes more ER use, but whether there is any relationship between care coordination assignment and ER use. The design allows you to explore multiple potentially contributory variables. The primary outcome variable for this question isn't the clinical condition; it is ER utilization.

Now you select the question for your study. You find that information is available from hospitals with and without care coordination teams.

Identify the study variables

Now you want to list all the possible variables needed to address the study question. Table 1 contains a list of some of the possible variables you could include.

Table 1: Potential variables for pediatric asthma patients ER utilization	
Gender	Age
Race and Ethnicity	Family size (siblings)
Living/housing status	Exposure to secondhand smoke
History of ER visits pre and post care coordination team assignment	Number of days in day care Other variables that might trigger an asthmatic event
Length of time since diagnosis	Medications
Asthma severity ratings outpatient and ER	Other environmental or seasonal exposures

Consider the scope and size of the project

Strictly speaking, to keep the project simple and small, all you need is whether the child is or is not assigned a care coordination team and the frequency of ER visits.

You could stop there so long as you have a specific point in time you are measuring. If you collect information on ER use for the previous twelve months, you will want to have cases of children assigned to the care coordination team prior to those twelve months and a sample of cases who never have a team assignment.

If you want to explore whether other variables may influence ER use within each group, you might include gender and age as well as the length of time since diagnosis and asthma severity ratings. This makes your study more sensitive. It is important to consider your variables with respect to those used in similar studies, but also to resist having too many variables.

Every variable you want to include must be defined. For example, age would be age at time of study, or date of birth. Days in day care can be weekly or monthly. How will you define the family, number of siblings, and living and housing conditions for the study subject? Can you get information on family size? You will need to perform this process for every variable.

Answer the questions:

- How will you define it?
- How will you code it?
- Are the data available in the format that you used to define the variables?

Compare your list to the literature

After you have a list of variables, the next step is to compare your list to a few recently published studies on this topic using the same or similar question you have selected for your project.

Template 6. Critical Analysis of a Research Report has 27 items that will guide you through identifying and recording the key elements of a research study. The information you will record in this template helps you identify similarities between the published study you are analyzing, and your project. When you evaluate the information, you will be able to generate a substantial list of possible study variables to include or exclude in your project. Comparing your list to those in the study or studies on which your project rests may generate additional variables, or possibly eliminate some.

Review the list with an expert

An extra opportunity to boost the strength of your study, and perhaps its value, would be to review the list with an expert, someone who works with pediatric asthma patients and knows what data are available and in what form. Ask them what they think about your list and what they would change.

So, let's say you have your list and you've checked it out with the literature, collected other opinions, and made necessary revisions. Now is the time to *consider if you need to refine your question*. Why? Because if you have too many variables, it will be difficult to collect and manage the data or to detect a meaningful or statistically significant effect. If you have too few because they are not all available, your study will be unreliable. We'll look more at these issues in Chapters Five and Seven.

Measures and Statistical Considerations
(Templates 9 and 11)

Meet with a biostatistician. Even though it is a little early in the process of constructing a complete project plan, you can hold a preliminary meeting with a biostatistician. Most projects require at least two meetings, some more than two.

A doctorate prepared biostatistician? I recommend this level of training for healthcare students if such a person is available. Of course, this will depend on your academic institution's faculty structure.

A master's prepared statistician? A seasoned expert in health research will be most helpful in the analysis and presentation phase.

Both of these statistical experts should be individuals who are willing to work closely with you to think critically about your design and methods. This will require an investment of their time and yours.

The first meeting should cover at least three items: get help clarifying and defining study variables, get an idea of the number of study subjects or cases you need, and discuss the analysis approach. This meeting can provide greater clarity and meaning to your project and ground it in the most suitable statistical structure.

Thinking about your study question in the context of the variables you have chosen is a method of double-checking the strength of the question. You will avoid future problems armed with the technical guidance a biostatistician can provide on the nature of the variables, your ability to quantify them, and the way they will guide the analysis. You might decide on a primary variable and secondary variable sets.

Consider their familiarity with your field. He or she should be someone who works with other researchers in your field or a closely related field. If your interest is in social sciences, a biostatistician who works with clinical trials might be compatible. By the same token, a biostatistician who works with basic science lab research might not be as well suited to a project in a healthcare-related field.

What You Want to Get from Consulting with a Biostatistician

As I said, there are three reasons to meet with a biostatistician.

The first is to finalize a list of variables. The second is to determine the number of study subjects or cases needed to confidently analyze the data. The third is to clarify the analysis approach.

The challenges of understanding how variables are classified can be resolved in a discussion with a statistician who is conversant with health research topics. Variables in a study can be classified in different ways according to their use and their suitability for statistical tests. Study variables may be called data, and their characteristics or qualities may be called data points, or properties.

In my colleague Jim Frost's book *Introduction to Statistics,* he defines types and subtypes of data that will help you determine what type of variables you will be measuring in your study. You can find his book at: *https://statisticsbyjim.com/* where you'll be certain to have understandable and accurate definitions.

Briefly, you should know that data are generally classified into quantitative and qualitative. Within those broad types, there are subtypes, including continuous (interval and ratio) and discrete (nominal and ordinal).

A nominal variable would be, for example, gender (male or female) or race (Asian, Black, and Caucasian).

Ordinal variables have a value assigned as a number on a range, such as hot or very hot, or a range of responses on a survey question such as strongly agree and strongly disagree.

Interval scales include a meaningful distance between any two points, but there is no zero denoting the absence of the characteristic.

Ratio data has the same properties as interval data, and has a specified zero. Examples of ratio data are dose amounts, weight, and length.

Consult Jim Frost's book for more discussion about types of variables and their use and application in statistics.

What do you need for this meeting? *Template 9, Biostatistician Meeting Checklist* can be used to document the information from the meeting and guide the agenda.

Benchmark Studies Your biostatistician will need information from one or two published studies that are most like yours. Let's call them benchmark studies, as they will set certain parameters for your project.

S/he will depend on your understanding of the area of study.

Although you have not completed your formal literature search, you have used the literature in your field to create your study question. Select one or two published research studies that are most like your project, with the same study population and outcome variables, or conditions of interest. Preferably that study's question or aim was the same as yours.

From these articles, using *Template 6*, you can locate the specific elements of your project you will need to have available to achieve maximum benefit from these meetings with a biostatistician.

Don't worry if you do not have these elements in your toolkit at this point. You may need to wait until you complete your literature search because for your project you may not have your final question and all the statistical benchmarks of a study that is most similar to yours. Sometimes the final study question emerges after the literature search is completed.

For your convenience, I have included this same information in Chapter Seven, Structure & Methods.

Here is the information you need from one or two benchmark studies.

1. Primary outcome variable,
2. Number of cases in that study,
3. The statistical test used,
4. The effect size, and
5. The P-value. *(P-values indicate the strength of the evidence against the null hypothesis. Lower values indicate stronger evidence. When the evidence is strong enough, you can reject the null hypothesis.)*

The agenda for a meeting with a biostatistician would cover at least the following decision points. Remember that struggling with these issues is normal. You aren't stupid. You know your field of study. Your statistical advisor knows theirs. Trust your advisor to help you work through the concepts. Rely on them to do the math with you. That is why the choice of a stats advisor is a crucial element in crafting your research plan.

- Refinement and finalization of variable definitions (Specific Aims, Background & Importance, and Methods)
- Becoming confident that what you are collecting is what you want to measure, not a surrogate for it, unless it has been found to be reliable. (Methods)
- Determining if you need a certain number of cases to analyze the data in ways that will answer your question or accurately test your hypothesis, and how many. (Power Analysis)
- Determining which statistical tests are best suited to those types of data, or types of variables, while answering the question you have posed. (Methods)
- Identification and description, to the extent needed, the statistical software you will use. (Methods)

Jim Frost's text on *Hypothesis Testing* can be found at: *https:// statisticsbyjim.com/hypothesis-testing/*

Below is a link to a paper on calculating effect sizes from published research articles by Thalheimer & Cook.

http://www.bwgriffin.com/gsu/courses/edur9131/content/Effect Sizes_pdf5.pdf

Be sure to keep your advisor in the loop on these interactions with the statistics side of the house.

Data Collection Considerations

After you have your complete list of variables fully defined and categorized, it is important to begin thinking about the steps involved in collecting your data.

It's better to think about this early in the project development and consider any potential obstacles to collecting all the information you need. Ask yourself whether you can collect and manage all these data.

**Why is it important to consider data management
at this point?
Because if you don't do it now, you may go too far down a
path that has a dead-end.**

First, whatever you cannot collect may limit the validity of your findings, and your results or answers to the question.

Second, if for some reason you cannot acquire all the data for all subjects, you need to consider if that will limit your study too much to be meaningful or valid. There will be missing data or gaps, making analysis difficult.

Third, if your design requires a minimum number of cases or data points to test the null hypothesis, you must be able to collect information to meet the requirement.

If your find that you can access, collect, and manage all the information you need for all the variables, you are ready to begin crafting sections of the plan.

As part of the process of constructing the Structure & Methods section, in Chapter Seven, I've provided *Template 11. Data Collection and Management.*

To wrap up this chapter, here is one more example of the mental processes that help to formulate a measurable study question.

Quality of life in patients at high risk for hospital readmission

1. Observe

To slow the rising cost of healthcare, hospitals in my city have started using health advisors (patient navigators and community health workers) to follow up with discharged patients at risk of readmission.

2. Speculate

Besides reducing the risk of readmission due to an exacerbation of the illness for which they were hospitalized, I'm interested in whether there are unexpected benefits for patients who utilize the services of a community health worker (CHW) program.

3. Question

Do CHW programs improve health outcomes?

4. Validate

This question is very broad. You do more research into the topic.

Upon investigating journal articles about CHW program outcomes, you find different types of CHW programs serving different communities, populations, and health conditions. You discover that all four hospitals in your city offer at least one CHW program, three of them are for diabetes patients, two are for heart disease patients, and one is for children with asthma. There are two that serve primarily, but not exclusively, Hispanic communities. Participation is not required. One of the Hispanic community CHW programs offers incentives for participation.

5. Observe with increased focus

While there are sufficient numbers of patients participating in CHW programs from the Hispanic communities to ensure study validity, you realize that none of these programs have been compared on readmission rates or other variables such as patient satisfaction or other health outcomes. The programs for adult patients all have the same services, with one providing participation incentives. Recall there are three specifically for diabetic patients. That program classifies the patients according to a risk rating scale.

6. Speculate with increased focus

It seems possible that CHW programs for diabetes patients might differ on readmission rates and other outcomes, particularly because of the mixed racial and ethnic populations being served.

7. Question with increased focus

What are the readmission rates for Hispanic women with diabetes who participate in a CHW program?

8. Validate to narrow the question

With additional reading, you find that some studies suggest that patient satisfaction may be a key to continued participation in CHW programs. Research also indicates that outcomes differ by race and ethnicity.

9. Consider data availability

You can get data on readmissions for patients participating in the five adult CHW programs. The programs regularly collect patient satisfaction surveys.

10. Question reformulation

Based on all the information, there are several questions you can ask to compare outcomes between groups.

a. Do readmission rates for Hispanic women with diabetes differ from CHW participants from other racial and ethnic groups?
b. Are readmissions rates lower overall for incentivized patients?
c. Is patient satisfaction related to readmission rate?
d. Do patient satisfaction rates differ among CHW participants on the basis of age, socioeconomic status, race, or ethnicity?

11. Validate

You find a recent study that measured patient satisfaction and quality of life, and included other health outcome measures. Upon inquiry, you find that all the CHW programs collect quality of life and certain clinical measures of wellness every six months. There are data available to you for the past two years.

12. Finalize measurable question

Returning to your original idea of whether quality of life is impacted by participation in a CHW program, and keeping in mind that the CHW program cannot *cause* a change in quality of life, you might be able to answer one of these two questions:

    a. Do patients in the CHW program report an improvement in their quality of life before and after participating? (Cohort, one group)

    b. Does quality of life differ for CHW program participants on the basis of disease type, gender, age, race, or ethnicity? (Correlational, more than one group)

13. Consider data availability for questions a and b above

For Question a: Maybe the CHW program already collected quality-of-life information before the person enrolled, and you could acquire those data and collect a second questionnaire to determine changes in one group.

Possibly the program has multiple quality-of-life scores at intervals that you can collect and analyze.

Whichever it is, you can include variables of demographics, living arrangements, medical diagnoses, and changes in health status.

For Question b: You will need to collect quality-of-life information for a group who opted out of the CHW program. In this situation, you would want to ensure your two groups were as similar as possible on demographic variables, strengthening the validity of your study.

NOTE: Research helps us to acquire a better understanding of an observed phenomenon, not to predict that one event causes a specific outcome, but to evaluate the strength of a relationship between an event and an outcome. Research does not definitively prove anything.

Therefore, avoid asking a question that implies causation. There are methods for identifying predictor variables, but they rely on the strength of a relationship, not a causation. We cannot reasonably determine absolutely whether something causes something else. We can determine whether an event is related to an outcome.

To construct a null hypothesis for testing, convert a question to a statement that reflects what you do **not** think will be the result.

Four additional examples of measurable questions for feasible projects in different fields

Leadership

Many studies are published about leadership style, the qualities of a good leader, and qualities of specific types or positions of leadership. A research question might arise about whether the qualities of U.S. presidents differ during wartime compared to peacetime. A hypothesis might be: *U.S. presidents during wartime are more likely to be autocratic in their leadership styles compared to U.S. presidents during peacetime.* This study could be conducted using a focused review of the literature project structure.

Decision-making

You think nursing supervisors are more autocratic in their supervision style than physician supervisors seem to be. You wonder if different professions might tend toward different preferred decision-making styles. A measurable question might be: *Is the professional affiliation of supervisors at university health center associated with a specific decision-making style?* A hypothesis might be: *More nurse supervisors use an autocratic style of decision-making than a participatory style.* For this type of cross-sectional study, you might mail or distribute electronic questionnaires to a large sample of nursing supervisors around the United States.

Water Intoxication

How much water produces intoxication? Would a quantity, based on certain conditions, answer this question? How much water produces intoxication in a person on antipsychotic medications? This question can be measured, possibly in a focused review of the literature, differentiating the specific medications as variables. Typically, however, this would beg a natural experimental or quasi-experimental study design.

Presenting problems at admission to a psychiatric hospital

Are presenting problems at inpatient admission similar among males with treatment-resistant schizophrenia, with and without personality disorder traits? You want to know if the reasons for admission differ between two different diagnostic groups of male patients. In terms of study design, you want to know if, at the time of admission, males with schizophrenia and personality disorder traits have different reasons for admission than males with schizophrenia and no personality disorder traits. You will assess them "at the same point in time" (i.e., at the admission event). Consider a cross-sectional or possibly case-control design.

Factors associated with adherence to a physical therapy regimen

Does education mediate the severity of injury and adherence to a physical therapy (PT) regimen? You want to know if the completed degree or number of years of education is related to both a severity of an injury (requiring or amenable to PT) and the extent to which the person follows the PT plan. Consider a correlational study design.

— FIVE —

The Literature Search

Overview

It is unclear exactly how many scientific journals there are, but estimates suggest that over one million scientific articles are published each year. These days, most foreign language articles are available in English, and some journals offer open access. If your advisor is satisfied with your using only the open access literature, you can consider that, of course. However, you should be aware of the limitations of such a search.

This chapter guides you through the process of conducting a deep literature search, one that enables you to focus your study lens on the important sources. It provides tools for evaluating the material, and for keeping only the research reports that pertain directly to your study. It also covers how to develop and shape your study question using the literature. A "Lit Search" is related to all three major sections of the Plan: Specific Aims, where you summarize the current knowledge from studies you selected, and its relevance to your study; the Background & Importance section, where you identify the most relevant works and discuss how they support your project ideas; and Structure & Methods, where you rely on previous research to strengthen the structure and methods for your project.

Consider the lit search in relationship to the Specific Aims. You may have been inspired by an article on the future of nursing care that you came across in a class or journal club about post-partum depression or psychiatric diagnoses in different races and ethnic groups. You may have been intrigued by some fact you read about cancer survivors or the effects of diet and exercise on mood and human performance. The literature search will uncover and reveal information that helps you craft the rationale for your project.

You can begin with a broad question and read more articles about the topic. Consider reading a few of the articles cited by the authors of the one that first attracted your interest. As you read them, think about how the questions they generated for future exploration and whether you might pursue one of those questions. Using a study question from a published article in a study of local conditions, for example, is certainly permissible with all appropriate citations and credits.

Additional reading doesn't, unfortunately, constitute a formal literature search. However, there are ways you can prepare for conducting the search that will save time in the long run.

Before you start the search: Step One (Template 4)

Below, I've listed seven questions for you to answer *before you start your search*. Attending to these questions will help you to be efficient, saving time and avoiding stress. In Appendix 3, you will find *Template 4. The Literature Search: Nine Points of Preparedness* for filling in your answers to these questions.

1. Address whether there are existing "reviews of the literature" on your topic. If there are, begin with those.
2. Are there textbooks or chapters in published textbooks on this subject, in addition to published peer review articles? Get copies of those for your binder.
3. Would unpublished material exist on this topic that you should consider (e.g., policies, minutes of meetings, or papers) that may help my review?
4. Is there an underlying theoretical or contextual framework that defines your topic of interest?
5. What keywords will you use for the first scan through the literature?
6. Do you have an electronic file system ready to populate?
7. Do you have a checklist for evaluating strengths and weaknesses of the materials?

What other ways can you prepare for an efficient literature search?

What can you do to prepare for an efficient literature search? Before you dive into reading too much, become more broadly acquainted with the published literature most closely associated with your research question.

Start by reading a few randomly selected articles on the topic. Just remember that reading a few articles does not constitute a literature search.

You can also acquaint yourself with prominent researchers in your field. Find their published research. Contact them and seek their advice. Most authors and researchers are happy to inspire others.

Become familiar with articles by referring to the first author's last name, such as the article by Ender, or Ender's article.

In the process of reading in your chosen field or topic, be sure to think about the literature as material for shaping and refining your study question.

If a question comes to you about something you're studying or reading, write it down, and look at the literature to determine if anyone else has asked that same question. Maybe someone has, but maybe you have a different perspective.

Preliminary Scouting (Template 5)

Five considerations for determining the value of source material to your study

I've provided a guide in the form of five considerations for you to evaluate the extent to which the articles meet your needs and constitute a solid foundation for collecting additional literature or source materials. These five considerations break down, in detail, the thought process that occurs in making decisions about the value of source materials, including research articles, textbooks, and reports. Work slowly, responding to every question within each consideration, and following the action steps. *Template 5. Source Materials: Five Considerations* is a fillable form for your use in this process.

Step 1. Identify and acquire the pdfs or printed copies of no more than three of the most recently published studies directly associated with your topic or question.

Step 2: Read them. Be sure you understand the analysis and findings for each study. Seek counsel if you stumble over any material.

Step 3: Refer to these articles to respond to the five considerations.

Eventually, your mind will work quickly, almost automatically, through the process prescribed by these five considerations.

Consideration #1: Can I use these articles for the following four plan development tasks?

Task a. Refining my study question
Task b. Supporting the importance of my project
Task c. Selecting a suitable design or structure for my project
Task d. Assessing the need for a power analysis, number of cases or subjects, and data analysis methods

The following information should be in the articles.

□ Topic   □ Design

□ Study question or aim   □ Methods

□ Population   □ Analysis

□ Sample size   □ Limitations

□ Primary outcome   □ Findings

□ Measurement instruments detailed   □ Significance

□ Variables   □ Effect size

□ Intervention or hypothesized explanatory variable (optional)

Action Step: Determine your next step using the following criteria.
    Criterion 1. If all the necessary information is not contained in the articles, refine your search terms or your question.
    Criterion 2. If there is sufficient information in at least one article, discard the others, and proceed to Consideration #2.
    Criterion 3. If only some of the information directly relates to

your study question, you can try to address the remaining four considerations, but before you do, consider the citations in those articles,
acquire two or three, review those, and return to consideration #1.

Example: You've found a study of factors contributing to
recovery in post knee arthroscopy athletes, but your interest is in
knee replacement, and in a variety of age groups. What should you
do? You can keep the article, examine the citations to determine if
there is a study more similar to your interest and focus, find them
and review them, (action step) then discard this study.

*When you have at least two articles with all the information that
relates specifically and directly to your project, and you have satisfied the
first consideration, proceed to address Consideration #2.*

Consideration #2: Do these articles support and/or justify the
purpose of my project and the question I have formulated? Does the
information help me with the structure & methods of my project?
Can I use them for comparing my results? Do they provide adequate
evidence that makes a compelling case that my study has value?

Action Step

If they **do not** meet the requirements, revise your study question
and refine your search terms. Then begin again at Consideration #1
with your new materials.

If they **do** meet the requirements, proceed to Consideration #3.

Consideration #3: Does it appear that any of the sources cited by
the authors in these studies would also be important to include and
useful for constructing the study plan?

a) Using the authors' citations, locate the ones most germane to
   your question and any that were seminal works (foundational,

groundbreaking). Acquire those articles and read the abstracts. Then address items *b* and *c* below.

b) Consider the conclusions for each article to determine whether your question addresses a relevant aspect of previous findings, to identify trends in the research, and to refer to recommendations for future directions.

c) Review the authors' identified knowledge gaps and their recommendations for further research. Be sure that you have not missed a more recent paper with additional research on the topic.

Consideration #4: Are there additional articles that would be helpful, or can I stop here?

(NOTE: If your mentor or course requires an exhaustive search, or if your mentor has published in this topic, you may need to continue to acquire articles/materials.)

Before you decide to stop your search, consider a and b below.

a) Consider reviewing information on fact-based, reliable, and valid web-based sources such as national, state, or local statistics or reporting agencies.

b) When you start seeing citations or articles repeated in your search, you probably have exhausted the most relevant available publications on this topic.

Consideration #5: Do I have sources of contradictory viewpoints on this topic? If you do not, you should explore whether materials exist that conflict with, refute, oppose, or dispute the importance of or direction of this line of study. If they do exist, you should explore them. *Don't overlook the possibility that, for example, if there are no more articles about family stress factors and childhood cancer, there may be studies of family stress factors and other childhood diseases or conditions.*

Remember as you review materials, that you want an unbiased

reader of your Background & Importance section to conclude that your review of the literature is **relevant, appropriate, thorough, and usful for your research project**. You want the reader to say: "Oh, wow! I see why this is important."

Conducting the Literature Search

SAVE TIME – ORGANIZE FIRST!

A well-organized, focused, goal-oriented approach will save you a lot of time as you search the literature.

First: Using the source materials from the preliminary scouting activity, draft a literature search outline. Use questions rather than statements, or use a brainstorming or mind mapping method. You can put into the outline all the questions that remain that you could answer with additional source materials.

If your outline consists of more than three or four questions, you could be overthinking or you might be unclear about your study focus.

Be sure your question is well defined, even if it is based in the literature or in other texts. Those sources do not constitute your formal literature background source materials for the B&I section of the plan.

Second: Talk with faculty members, biostatisticians, and librarians about your outline.

Talk to them, out loud, about your premise, your idea, the three foundational articles you have read, and your question that arises from your curiosity about events or conditions you've observed or about which you've heard.

Third: Revise the outline based on their input, and begin the search.

You might keep your original outline with added notes. You might refine your outline statements. You might modify your study aim, focus, and question.

- A literature search means just that. It's a search. So, search multiple sources.
- Use a combination of methods. (For various methods, consult with librarian.)

The most useful combination might include a literature database search (e.g., Pub-Med, specific journals, National Center for Biotechnology Information), direct contact with the author of a paper, and examination of citations in relevant articles or texts.

Organizing the Tasks and the Materials

Step 1. Use of literature and other search engines: Take time to understand how to use the database. Search engines and databases are robust and complex. Most electronic compendia of literature, texts, papers, and other materials offer options for focusing your search using multiple different key word variations. Many journal articles include key words that attach to or link to the topic of that article. If you have no clear direction of your own, you can use those as a starting point.

Step 2. Limit the number of articles: If you are writing a dissertation, or a manuscript, you may require an exhaustive search. For a small, non-experimental study project, you can use published studies from the last two years, and the foundational work as appropriate. If you find more than twenty articles on your topic, without exhausting the supply, try refining your search terms with more precise, specific keywords or phrases.

Here are some strategies to keep only the most important references, and ensure they are the most relevant to your project.

a. Eliminate studies that do not use the same study population, the same outcome variables, and the same study design as you will use, unless even if you have a study on the topic with a different population, or more variables than you are considering, the information may nonetheless, enrich your discussion of available knowledge of your population.*

b.*Some healthcare topics and some populations are less researched than others, resulting in a paucity of literature on that subject, and serendipitously leaving the topic wide open for you to explore.*

Step 3. Apply revised or new keywords: Enter a new set of keywords or new authors or follow links provided in the citations.

Step 4. Select and evaluate three to five of the most recently published studies: Be certain that you understand what the researchers did, with what subjects and what data, the limitations and strengths of the designs, and the conclusions before you conclude that these studies are suitable to include as tools in your project.

Step 5. Read the abstracts online. Of course, you can print the abstracts, but avoid printing numerous articles until you are sure you want them printed. That could waste resources.

Step 6. Keep searching if needed, following the citations in those articles, or refining your study question.

Step 7. Track back: After you have three to five (try to limit it to only three) of the most recently published studies that are **directly** related to your project, track back chronologically, or logically, to trace the history and development of the topic to the seminal research in the area if appropriate.

Step 8. Branch out:

a. Include at least one seminal study or theory building article in this topic, regardless of its age. That may mean dipping into the literature of the 1960s or 1940s depending on your topic and whether you have a theoretical framework you must explain or justify.

b. Include any meta-analyses as well as focused or critical reviews of the topic.

c. Include foreign articles—you can get translations if you need, and software is available to translate most languages.

d. Include research that disputes your speculation. If your interest is in women's health, review the same area of research in men. Perhaps women are understudied in that area. That information may help support the rationale for your project.

Step 9. Evaluate the three most recently published works using the five considerations for determining the value of source material to your study, if you have not done it before now.

Step 10. Create a compendium of source materials with five to ten articles from the types above. Limit your compendium first to the research papers you understand.

Step 11. Create an electronic file with topic-labeled file folders. Be specific rather than general in labeling the file folders. This makes it easier to find an article. For example, instead of a single folder labeled "Women and Depression," use "Women and Depression" for a folder and inside have more specific topic-labeled files such as "post-partum and race," "perinatal factors," "access to care and culture," and so on as applicable.

Step 12. Read the complete article electronically, taking notes in an organized spreadsheet file by author's last name.

Alternatively, you can print the articles and mark them with highlighters and handwritten notes in the margins or on a separate lined page. If you print articles, organize them in a three ring notebook, separated with alphabetical tabs with the last name of the first author and the date of publication on each tab. Always make a list by last name of first author to put in the front of the binder for quick reference. Or number them and use a numerical table of contents in the front of the binder.

Here is an example of column headings you could use on a spreadsheet.

Primary Author's Last Name	Author's Initials	Date: Year/ Month	Journal Name; Volum, Issue, Page numbers	Title	Key Words	Notes

In spreadsheet software, you can organize your notes by sorting them by column headings. Another reliable method is to keep handwritten 3x5 index cards (front and back) to prompt your recollection of the study details. You can prioritize and group them by color or by topic to keep the most important ones front and center.

Example index card or electronic note

Author	Journal, year, volume, and page nums
Topic/Focus	
Title	
Aim - Primary Question/Hypothesis	
Data source(s)	
Structure/Design and Methods	
Results/Findings	
Limitations	
Recommendations for future research/action	
Comments: unique features, stimulating facts	

Reviewing and Evaluating Source Materials (Templates 6 – 7)

In this part of Chapter Five, we'll consider two strategies for evaluating and analyzing research articles and other source materials you'll uses in developing your project. I'm using the term "source material" because you might include textbooks, websites, and other narrative materials outside of the peer-reviewed published research literature as references.

The first strategy is to critically analyze the materials. The second strategy is to perform an in-depth analysis of source materials.

The critical analysis is a more thoughtful approach to taking notes about a research article, than the second more in-depth strategy discussed below. A critical analysis is suitable for assessing the overall value of a research report. This strategy is more conceptual rather than structural. The ten questions below capture the essence of this strategy. Although not all the terminology in these questions will fit all the types of resources you may use, the intent of each question will apply universally.

In Appendix 3, you will find *Template 6. Critical Analysis of a Research Article* with 27 items. Those 27 items break down the 10 basic questions below into greater detail.

Ten Questions to Perform a Critical Analysis of Research Reference Materials

1. What is the study topic? What are its purpose, aim, goal, question and/or hypotheses, and what is the theoretical framework for this research?
2. Is the importance of the condition being studied, or the overall topic, clearly established? What is it?
3. What is the study design or approach to exploring the topic? How does it suit the question or the goal? Would any other design be suitable to address the issue or study question? Has the author clearly explained the methodologies used in the study? Are opposing views included?

4. If you wanted to know more about the study, could you find it based on information in the article? Where would you find it? Can you reproduce the study design? Alternatively, could you replicate the analysis of the topic?

5. Are the measurement and data collection tools documented as valid and reliable, or are methods adapted to fit this study? Explain.

6. Are appropriate and valid statistical methods used to answer the study question? What are they and how do they help answer the question?

7. What conclusions are most useful, and does the author speculate about or interpret study findings? As you consider the conclusions, can you deconstruct or trace the flow of the discussion? Are there gaps, or leaps in logic?

8. In what ways does this material contribute to our understanding of the observed phenomenon of interest or provide valuable information to the field?

9. What are the strengths and limitations of the study?

10. Does the material support your research? If it does, what information will you use to shape, construct, organize, and/or conduct your study?

The second strategy is to perform an in-depth analysis of source materials. An in-depth analysis is more structural than conceptual. It requires you to document the methodology of a study in greater detail, without making any value judgements about the material.

Template 7. In-Depth Analysis of Source Material has 33 items in six sections. In section one, there are eight items that are the minimum concerns you should address when selecting or keeping a reference for use in your background and importance narrative. *Template 7* is particularly useful for preparing a presentation or leading a discussion in a journal club event, or at a conference or educational event. If you are conducting a focused review of literature, you will want to have one of these long forms for each source.

The relationship of the literature search to the other sections of the plan

By now you can see that the literature search fuels the rationale for the project and provides information for selecting the appropriate study design or approach. From the literature search, you acquire knowledge of what we already know about the topic of your study. Available research findings shape the direction of your project so that it makes a contribution to the field, expands upon little-understood phenomena, or fills a gap in our knowledge.

It is possible to have too much literature and too many articles. With a narrow focus, you can reduce the size and scope of your materials. Select only the most relevant minimally essential source materials.

Unless you are conducting an *exhaustive review* of a topic as a project, critically evaluate the material. Exclude any material that may be interesting but superfluous, excessive, or redundant. Ask the question: "Does it add value or simply repeat information?"

Have fun, and enjoy the journey, but do not spend valuable time reading more just because it's interesting. Read to learn and to strengthen your project.

www.CartoonStock.com

"But is it content?"

SIX

Background & Importance Section

Overview

The Background & Importance (B&I) section communicates that you have done your due diligence, you know the territory, and your project is grounded in theory and previous credible research. Because the B&I section communicates relevant knowledge about the question you propose to address and why it is important, it can be a challenging section to write. Be sure to read Chapter XII on scientific writing.

How long should it be? The B&I section should be written in about 1½ pages, or about 750 words, in Times New Roman, 12pt font, single-spaced.

If your project is complex, you might use 1¾ pages, but if you write more than that, you haven't used your best judgement about what is essential information for the plan document. You may have more information than you will put in this section, but you can refer to it when you write your findings.

In a small project, there should be only one study question or aim.

However, if your topic has specific clinical paradigms or theories that should be partitioned, you can divide the B&I section into sub-topics or questions by using separate headings such as: "Stress and Coping in Children with Cancer and Their Families" and "Family Communication Styles."

In this section, you tell the reader what is in the literature, discuss it, make statements that link or talk about the relationships between and among the material, and conclude how this information supports the direction you are taking.

Include information that may contradict or contrast with your hypotheses. This is evidence that you are aware of these data and that you will address them. For example, if you are examining the efficacy of non-surgical interventions, discuss what is pertinent about surgical interventions for the same condition. If you are exploring issues related to depression in women, discuss the research on depression in males, and underscore how women are different and why your study does not include males. Using comparison groups or intricately related variables can provide rich descriptive narrative.

The process of writing the narrative B&I section helps you think carefully about the foundation of and rationale for your project. This is the opportunity to explore the topic of focus and how your project relates to the current available information from past research.

What Does the Background & Importance Section Include?

This section has two components. A review of the literature (or source materials) and an explication of the importance of your study. The importance is derived from how your study fills gaps, adds knowledge, or advances the field. It shows how the latest research on the topic supports your study aims. These elements are intertwined in the narrative that addresses ten points, woven together for a seamless presentation of the literature as it relates to your study. In the material below, I've listed the ten points and provided examples of how to address each point.

Guiding Principles

When you work with the ten points that must be covered in the B&I section, it will help you to use a few guiding principles.

Guiding Principles for Writing the Background & Importance Section
Be specific: guide the reader from the statement of your question or hypothesis into a discussion of its history and importance.
Populate each point with references to published studies or other source materials.
Use connective and conclusion phrases to move through the narrative.
Use contrasts, comparisons, and links between and among the studies you have chosen as most supportive and contradictory, if relevant, to your project.
Construct your responses using complete sentences. For each statement you make, refer to and cite the article where you found the information.

Ten Points

The following ten points need to be covered in the B&I section. Responding to each of these points will create material you can use to write the B&I section. *Template 8. Constructing the Background & Importance Section* is the fillable form you can complete with your own project-related material. At the end of this chapter, I've provided three examples of how to respond to each point.

1. What salient facts do we know about the topic?
2. State your study question and how it relates to those facts.
3. Describe the topic's scientific basis or principles, or its clinical or theoretical framework.
4. What did the seminal (original or groundbreaking) research contribute to the field, or how did it initiate the movement, framework, or theory?
5. What does the latest published research contribute to the topic, or how does it change what we know?
6. What are the gaps between what we know and what we need to know?
7. How will your study fill the gaps and improve knowledge or practice in the field?
8. What is the benefit to seeking additional knowledge to address this question? How does it help the field?
9. What does conflicting or contrasting research contribute to this topic?
10. What information supports the rationale for your study?

How to Construct the Background & Importance Section (Template 8)

Ten Points with Examples

Referring to the ten elements you just read, try to create a ten-point outline for your B&I section, with any sub-elements that you think are important for your project. Write your statements in *Template 8* or create your own outline.

You probably will draft it, edit it, and write it again. You may have some frustration with this section, and that is normal. Take a mental step back if you feel overwhelmed. Ask someone to review your B&I Construction Template, or read it aloud alone, and read it to someone.

It's quite possible that even on a third draft, your advisors may see something they did not see at first. That is why it is crucial to get other input and take breaks from your work to gain perspective, see the gaps in the information you've covered, or discover any thinking errors or contradictions in your material. Clear your head by taking a walk, watch part of a movie, take a nap, or meditate.

After creating narrative material that responds to each point, you should have enough content for a draft or an outline of your Background & Importance section.

Activity

Use your left-brain to draw lines between related thoughts or statements. Use your right brain to draft segue sentences or draw lines connecting the points so you can develop a logical discussion of the information. The discussion does not need to be chronological. It needs to be logical, with information grouped by connected or related elements of the studies you are reviewing. Your observations, facts, opinions, and reactions to the points you are covering need to connect seamlessly.

The impact of your statements and the connections you make between the observations will likely change over time. If you stay the course and complete a solid draft of the B&I section, the Structure & Methods section will be easier to write. Your thinking will become more coherent, and you will be better prepared to conduct and complete the project.

As you write the B&I section, focus on being succinct, coherent, powerful, and parsimonious.

Succinct – It's not a fishing pond. Be brief, use as few words as possible; stay on point, no extra verbiage.
Coherent – This is not a moving cloud formation. It all makes sense, becomes stable, and hangs together in one meaningful message.
Powerful – No need for a raging storm; but strong with an impact that makes you think.
Parsimonious – No, that's not a root vegetable, but it is the root of wise reductionism.

Preparing an Introduction to the Background & Importance Section

The B&I section needs an introductory statement before you launch in to the first of the ten points.

At this point in developing your research project plan, you may not have enough information to write the introductory statement for the B&I section. You can, nevertheless, draft it and keep revising it as you further develop your other narrative sections.

You will not finish the Specific Aims section until you have completed the Structure & Methods section, and this introductory statement should link the Specific Aims to the B&I section. It happens sometimes that a sentence in the middle of a paragraph stands out as a strong candidate for an introductory statement. Here are three segue examples.

Example 1

My interest in studying the role of self-esteem in recovery from depression in young women arises from the evidence that self-esteem is associated with childhood trauma, and childhood trauma is a precipitating factor in developing depression. Therefore, I propose to explore the relationship between resilience, childhood trauma, and self-esteem in a group of women, ages 25 to 30, who are recovering from depression. In the following material, I discuss existing knowledge of this relationship, and how it led to my study aims.

Example 2

This case-control study of stress and coping in families of children with cancer is supported by recent published studies. Innovative programs equipping these families with resiliency skills and abilities suggest that families' communication styles under stress may predict their responsiveness to resiliency interventions. The studies most relevant to this question are discussed below.

Example 3

The earliest research published on factors contributing to reading skills and abilities in grade school children was in 1960, when Smith et al. developed a social paradigm to assess literacy. Today, states have reading comprehension tests for all grade school age children. My study focuses on the question of whether student–teacher ratio is related to reading skills and abilities in sixth grade students. Recent studies, discussed below, point to this possibility, and I propose to test those theories in the local school districts.

Exercise: Thought processes accompanying the development of the Background & Importance section.

Thought: What if I have too much to put in the background? For example, I have twenty or more articles to cover in this section.

Reaction: In this case, consider confining your narrative to the studies published in the past two to three years. Describe in one or two sentences the plethora of studies in this arena, and how and why you selected certain studies to include in this section.

Above all, lead the reader to conclude that evidence from previous research does in fact directly support the value and structure of your project, or that the knowledge about the subject is insufficient and your project will add to that knowledge.

Thought: How do I communicate the topic's scientific basis or principles, or its clinical or theoretical framework?

For example: Do families of youth in juvenile detention facilities have similar styles of family communications? Or do family systems communication styles of youth in juvenile detention differ according to juvenile's type of criminal charges?

The first question is exploratory, describing with data the various styles used by families of juveniles in custody. The second question is more specifically aimed at classifying the cases by type of criminal charge (e.g., violent, nonviolent) and comparing the family systems communication styles of the two groups.

Reaction: Either way, the relevant theoretical frameworks are *Family Systems Theory* and *Communication Styles*. Summarize these theories, referring to the seminal (original, groundbreaking) work that created the theories.

Thought: I want to replicate a study. How do I write a Background & Importance section for a single study?

Reaction: If you have justifiable reasons to conduct a study that has already been done, for example, with a different population or with additional modifiers, describe what and whose study, and why. Discuss the theory or framework the original study used and how replicating it will add to our understanding of the topic or population.

If you expect to make this statement in the Specific Aims section, you can cover the literature or source materials most closely associated with the study you will replicate. The narrative may be brief, covering only the essential information needed to provide the backdrop and rationale for your project.

Thought: I want to develop a new instrument for measuring a condition in a population, such as quality of life, opinions about people with drug dependencies, or a test of knowledge about a topic.

Reaction: Make a clear statement about its value in this section, using published tests of a related topic, or the instrument you will modify or create anew.

For the ten points you will cover in the B&I section, I've provided three examples. These are fabricated examples. The material does not constitute material for or from an actual study. If any material is similar to an existing or future study, it is purely accidental.

EXAMPLE A. Do Medicaid patients have increased risk factors for slow recovery following knee surgery? (Correlational)

1. Write one or two sentences about the most important one to three facts we know about the topic.

   In the U.S., knee surgery occurs most often in persons ages 45 to 65. Obesity, diabetes, and arthritis are conditions that must be considered as risk factors in considering surgical interventions. Knee replacement surgeries tripled between 1996 and 2016, and Medicaid patients with this type of surgery may have longer hospital or rehabilitation lengths of stay.

2. Write a "therefore" sentence about your study question or aim.

   I propose to investigate whether patients with Medicaid

who are knee surgery candidates or have had knee surgery are more likely to have risk factors that may slow the recovery process.

As you work through the next eight points, you may decide that you want to refine your study question. By the time you finish the next eight items with your own project information, you may have actually done just that.

3. Describe the topic's scientific basis or principles, or its clinical or theoretical framework.

Orthopedic surgery for knee replacement considers co-existing clinical conditions as factors in recovery rates but not a combination of clinical conditions and insurance coverage. This study will examine recovery risk factors in Medicaid patients with diabetes.

4. If there is seminal research, what were the origins, the era, the impetus, and why has its contribution endured?

The first published research information I found on this question was in 1962. Authors found that surgical interventions should be tailored to the patient's resiliency. (Citation et al., 1962) The latest published information is from 2018. There is one review of the literature in 2012 that I used to refine my study question based on gaps in our knowledge of factors in knee surgery recovery. In that report, researchers indicate that we need further reflection on factors that may speed recovery in certain age groups.

5. Move into the published research you have found: What are the most salient results from the most recently published studies?

Name first author, et al., found that if recovery from knee surgery is difficult or takes too long, fatigue may dispose the person to other adverse conditions. Further, if a person does not regain full mobility, they may be at risk for depression or other physical injuries. (Citation, date) Therefore it is important to integrate these considerations into the care plan, and to tailor rehabilitation goals according to the individual's expectations and potential.

6. What, if any, conflicting or contrasting research or information pertains to this topic?

Findings on studies of recovery factors for post knee surgery patients vary depending on whether the study includes only physical or also considers psychosocial factors.

7. What gaps exist between what we know and what we need to know, and what would the field gain from more information?

We do not know whether risk of death is a crucial and necessary pre-surgical consideration. It remains unclear whether the extent of the pre-intervention deterioration of the joints impedes post-treatment recovery.

8. How will your study fill the gaps and improve knowledge or practice in the field?

This study will help local hospitals to improve their assessment of knee surgery candidates' pre-intervention health status to determine the best course of post-surgical services.

9.What is the benefit to seeking additional knowledge to address this question? How does it help the field?

Knowing what factors are associated with rapid and full, and slow and partial, recovery offers healthcare providers another dimension to consider in their treatment planning.

10.What information supports the rationale for your study?

Previous research underscores the importance of considering the whole patient even when the primary focus of the healthcare provider is on one part of the body.

EXAMPLE B. Do three elements of care—treatment responsiveness, mortality, and other negative health events—differ between patients with Community versus Hospital Acquired Pneumonia? (Correlational)

1.Write one or two sentences about the most important one to three facts we know about the topic.

The classification of pneumonia is complicated by the different etiologies. Under the most recent guidelines for diagnosing and treating pneumonia, there are four types defined as Community-Acquired (CAP), Healthcare Associated (HCAP), Hospital Acquired (HAP), and Ventilator-Associated (VAP). HCAP has a community-based etiology, slightly different in its exposure nature from CAP. HCAP has been observed as treatment resistant and may place a person at risk for other negative health events. Furthermore, information about mortality rates varies across studies for all types of pneumonia.

2.Write a "therefore" sentence about your study question
or aim.

I proposed to explore existing data on patients admitted to
three local hospitals with diagnoses of HCAP and CAP
to determine if there are differences in three elements of
care: evidence of treatment resistance, mortality, and other
negative health events.

*As you work through the next eight points, you may decide that you want
to refine your study question. By the time you finish the next eight items
with your own project information, you may have actually done just that.*

3.Describe the topic's scientific basis or principles, or its clinical
or theoretical framework.

Pneumonia is a complex disease process, occurring in all
age groups with risk for death or other infections. Clinical
information and guidelines change either too slowly or too
quickly, leading to confusion about diagnosis and evidence-
based treatment options. On a global scale, CAP is the
third most common cause of death.

4.If there is seminal research, what were the origins, the era,
the impetus, and why has its contribution endured?

Not applicable. Thus, you would either not address this
point or state that there is no seminal research per se on
this topic.

5.Move into the published research you have found: What are
the most salient results from the most recently published
studies?

Recent studies suggest that the timing of treatment for hospitalized patients with pneumonia is a factor in mortality. Furthermore, the scoring systems to classify a patient as treatment resistant or at high or low risk for death have been questioned. Most studies consider medical factors but not psychosocial or personal factors. In 2017, Smart et al. found differences in mortality risk scores for 350 patients hospitalized with HCAP and CAP, with CAP patients at higher risk. However, there are few studies that consider factors other than clinical tests. One study by Severia et al. included demographic, socioeconomic, and lifestyle factors. That study found that education, diet, and hygiene may be contributing factors in both CAP and HCAP.

6. What, if any, conflicting or contrasting research or information pertains to this topic?

The challenge in studying risk factors for mortality from CAP or HCAP is not conflicting information, but insufficient or inconsistent information.

7. What gaps exist between what we know and what we need to know, and what would the field gain from more information?

There are effective treatments for HCAP and CAP, but the physician must consider each patient's risk factors that may exacerbate the pneumonia or place them at risk for adverse events. Furthermore, the tendency to diagnose HCAP or CAP may mask other potential and more plausible diagnoses.

8. How will your study fill the gaps and improve knowledge or practice in the field?

This study will add to our knowledge about psychosocial factors associated with response to treatment, mortality, and negative health events for patients with CAP and HCAP.

9. What is the benefit to seeking additional knowledge to address this question? How does it help the field?

As the second most common nosocomial infection, pneumonia carries mortality risks. Healthcare professionals would benefit from knowing about patients' other risk factors for complications.

10. What information supports the rationale for your study?

Available studies emphasize the importance of continuous learning about how different persons respond to treatment for CAP and HCAP. Increased awareness of psychosocial factors affecting treatment responsiveness may prepare healthcare providers to more effectively mitigate negative outcomes.

EXAMPLE C. Do stress and coping differ in patients and families with Ewing Sarcoma compared to any other type of cancer? Are stress and coping strategies associated with family communication styles? (Exploratory, Correlational)

1. Write one or two sentences about the most important one to three facts we know about the topic.

When a child has cancer, the focus is on the child. But cancer also lays a burden on the entire family. The literature overall is confusing and inconsistent regarding the ways children and families cope with this disease burden. As survival rates improve, more children will go on to become adults and may continue to carry the burden. This begs the question of resilience. One reason for the confusion and inconsistency may be related to the type of cancer.

2. Write a "therefore" sentence about your study question or aim.

Therefore, this study has two aims: 1) to describe stress levels and coping strategies used by children, siblings, and parents in two groups, one with Ewing Sarcoma and the other with any other form of cancer; 2) to determine if the family communication style is associated with stress levels and coping styles.

As you work through the next eight points, you may decide that you want to refine your study question. By the time you finish the next eight items with your own project information, you may have actually done just that.

3. Describe the topic's scientific basis or principles, or its clinical or theoretical framework.

Much work has been done on measurements of stress and coping for children, and for the family system overall. Akins et al. developed a questionnaire in 1995 that has been revised multiple times and is currently endorsed by relevant professional groups.

4.If there is seminal research, what were the origins, the era, the impetus, and why has its contribution endured?

The theoretical framework for stress and coping has roots in the late 1970s in the work of Seldom and Rarely. They created a paradigm used to this day to classify types of stress based on its origins, and styles of coping based on its physiological drivers. According to the latest studies, attention is being increasingly given to coping mechanisms for parents of children with cancer, but little attention is given to siblings or the family as a unit. The first article I located was exploratory, in 1998, from a socioeconomic perspective. (Here you would discuss the family communications model you will use.)

5. Move into the published research you have found: What are the most salient results from the most recently published studies?

Recovery for the child with cancer may partly depend on their family's health status, according to research by First Author et al. Further, researchers at Harvard note that healthcare personnel should be aware of the complete social structure affecting the child. (Cite article) Here you would discuss a few more relevant studies that used the measurements you are using and what they found that inspired you to develop your project.

6.What, if any, conflicting or contrasting research or information pertains to this topic?

There is no conflicting information in this area, but there is confusing information. For example, one article suggests that after the first year of the disease, parents report no impact on their relationship, but other studies suggest that trauma effects may be longer term. This may also affect other members of the family. There is little to no information about how stress and coping for cancer patients and their families are related to the family's communication style.

7.What gaps exist between what we know and what we need to know, and what would the field gain from more information?

Because the extent to which stress and coping may be related to the type of cancer, this is the first aim of my study, to determine if Ewing Sarcoma families differ from all other types of cancer families. My second aim takes this research to a new area of study that is to examine whether stress and coping strategies are associated with one of four types of family communication styles.

8.How will your study fill the gaps and improve knowledge or practice in the field?

This study will help further our understanding of whether a specific type of cancer is related to specific stress and coping strategies.

9.What is the benefit to seeking additional knowledge to address this question? How does it help the field?

If Ewing Sarcoma families differ in stress and coping from other cancer-type families, this would prompt further investigation of other variables that may characterize these families. Further, if family stress and coping is associated with family communication style, this would inspire additional research in how communication styles facilitate coping or may be related to higher or lower levels of stress.

10. What information supports the rationale for your study?

Previous studies have not compared stress and coping in different types of cancer conditions, nor have they examined relationships between stress and coping and family communication styles.

SEVEN

Structure & Methods Section

Overview

Following the narrative that sets the stage and provides the rationale for your project, the Structure & Methods section details the design or approach to the study question, and the tasks and activities necessary to answer it.

This is the technical part of the plan. It will vary according to the structure, scope, and nature of your study aims. Here is where analytic thinking is useful. You will need to review this section thoroughly, perhaps more than once, with the biostatistician of choice and your advisor.

The first portion of this section is the structure, the second is how you will implement that structure.

What Does the Structure & Method Section Include?

This section of the research project plan includes information about the study design or the approach you are taking to address the study question, and the details on activities you will undertake to conduct and complete the study.

Writing this section for a plan differs somewhat from writing it for a proposal or application for funding. This is the section you will use to apply for approval from the Institutional Review Board (IRB) to acquire and/or use personal health information on you human subjects/participants.

There are ten essential elements in the Structure & Methods Section narrative.

1. Introduction
2. The study design
3. Power analysis
4. The study population
5. Study variables
6. Data management and analysis
7. Project management plan
8. Study integrity
9. Human Subjects
10. Other study requirements

What Do I Need to Have to Construct the Structure & Methods Section?

As we noted above, there are ten essential elements in the Structure & Methods Section of the RPP.

Introduction: The Structure & Methods Section requires an introduction. That introduction serves to connect the Background & Importance section to the description of all the protocols and tasks required to conduct the project. In the introductory statement, you will link the structure and methods back to the study question/aim. Not only does this help a reader or reviewer to follow the threads of your project plan from question to analysis strategies, but it also helps you to remain faithful to your study question and ensure that you are consistent throughout the plan.

Study Design: You have a measurable question or aim for your project, from *Template 3*, and a study design suitable to address the question. Following the introduction to the Structure & Methods Section, you will plainly and directly restate the study design.

Power Analysis: For the power analysis and sample size, from meetings with a biostatistician, using one or two published research studies that have the same or similar question as you have for your project, and the same study design, variables, measurement instruments (or similar), and statistical tests, you have completed the below list of information. This information should be recorded in *Template 9. Biostatistician Meeting Checklist and Agenda*.

If you have not completed *Template 9*, refer to Chapter Four to complete the process.

1. Primary outcome variable, and
2. Number of cases in that study, and
3. The statistical test used, and
4. The effect size, and
5. The P-value.

Study Population, Study Variables, Data Management and Analysis: The information you entered into *Template 9* will provide material for these narratives. These three elements include: the description of your population of interest, with the inclusion and exclusion criteria clearly delineated, all the variables/data you will collect, how you will collect, record and secure and protect study data, and how you will analyze those data and interpret findings.

Project Management Plan: The information you entered into *Template 11. Data Collection and Management* will provide material for this narrative.

Study Integrity: For this narrative, refer to the information you entered into *Template 9*.

Human Subjects Protection: Your approved IRB protocol is the source for this narrative.

Other Study Requirements: Use your notes from meetings with your advisors, and any other issues you have identified in your templates, to construct any narrative needed according to the nature and requirements of your project.

How Is the Structure & Methods Section Organized?

Generally, the S&M section follows a logical sequence of describing each of the nine elements in detail.

Including the introduction, the outline looks like this.

1. Introduction
    a. Restate the research aims, question/s or hypotheses including a statement about the topic and the population.
    b. Mention the approach you using to achieve the study aims or address the question.
    c. Describe how this section is organized.
2. Study design or project structure
    a. What it is.
    b. Why you have selected this approach.
3. Power analysis
    a. How many cases or subjects are needed to have confidence in the study findings?
    b. If the study is not responsive to the power analysis, describe why and what other strengths the study has.
4. Cases or subjects
    a. Inclusion and exclusion/selection criteria
    b. How is the sample to be drawn, or recruitment or selection methods and protections. (Caution is advised on using "volunteers," as this introduces a bias to your project.) Address consents in the Human Subjects section.
5. Outcome measures – variables of interest
    a. What are the study variables and their definitions?

  b.Methods of data collection (Where are the data? How will you collect data? Interviews? Survey distribution and collection? Data collection forms? Data requests?)

The structure of the database must be compatible with the way a statistical test performs, or you will have to transform the data set. Invest the time to understand why the configuration of the data set can be your best flying dream or your worst nightmare.

 6. Data management and analysis
 7. Project management plan and timelines
 8. Study integrity, including strengths and limitations
 9. Human subjects' protection protocols or procedures
 10.Other issues or special considerations, conditions, or requirements for this study

Template 10. Structure & Methods provides a detailed outline you can complete with your responses each required nine parts of the S&M section of the plan. Some institutions may require that you have each part listed in your document, even though for some items you might use NA as the content.

How Do I Construct the Structure & Methods Section? (Template 10)

For your reference, I've provided an example of a narrative that could be appropriate for each element in the outline for this section of your project plan. This material is fictionalized and does not represent any known actual study.

1. Introduction and Organization of the Section

The purpose of this study is to explore the source and types of stress experienced by families of children with cancer, and how they respond to them. This study includes adults and children.

To increase our understanding of the stress and coping mechanisms of families with the burdens of childhood cancer, I will conduct a cross-sectional study of a sample of families whose children are in treatment at Timberline Cancer Center in Bashful, Utah.

In the following material, I will address the power analysis performed in preparation for the study, and describe the sample, the data sources, data collection methods, and data management and analysis strategies. I will also provide the timetable of activities that ensure this project is feasible and completed on time.

2. Study Design

For this study, I selected a cross-sectional design. It is best suited to address the study question because it provides a sample of families and their experiences in a slice of time.

3. Power Analysis

a. How many cases or subjects are needed to have confidence in the study findings?

At this point, you will refer to information in *Template 9*, from your meeting with a biostatistician, where you documented the power analysis and the number of cases you need to reach the power you desire. If it isn't possible to include a sufficient number of cases or individuals to avoid errors, you may have to justify the study as exploratory and use caution with non-parametric statistical tests.

You can control variability in your data by narrowing the inclusion and exclusion criteria for study subjects or cases. For example, you could use length of time since diagnosis or onset to narrow the variability in how long the family has been coping the disease burden. Or you might consider the extent to which the social support variable mitigates the stress scores. Strive for a sample size that allows you to identify an effect (a relationship) but not the smallest one.

Please remember this is not just a "numbers game." It is an intelligent perspective on what you think the statistics will show as the strongest relationship between stress and coping and disease burden, or inability to cope with stress and socio-economic status. Whatever your focused question is, it must be focused to be meaningful.

If the biostatistician says it is possible to achieve minimum power with your potential N cases for the study, work with her or him to craft this narrative section. It is short. Shorter than what you have just read.

b. Reasons why this study will not be responsive to this target number.

If you can avoid having to write this section, please do! While small studies such as a scholarly project might not require meeting study power thresholds, be sure your study has other value.

Remember that statistical tests require a minimum number of cases for results to be trusted.

Meaningful research is what you are aiming for. Learn something new that contributes to your field of study.

4. Cases or Subjects

Inclusion and Exclusion/Selection Criteria: e.g., the clinic serves 158 families each month. I aim to enroll a total of 40 families in the study between March 1, 2025, and May 31, 2025. No exclusion criteria apply.

Selection or recruitment methods and protections: Here describe how you will obtain a sample, or how you will consent and enroll participants in the study. Include any summary needed to reflect approved protocols for ensuring choice and privacy.

5. Variables

Outcome measures are the variables you are positing to be affected by a condition or event, such as opinions, test scores, coping strategies, or length of stay. You'll need to describe the instruments you will use and define the variables. You have previously explained the theoretical foundation of the measurements such as those for stress, coping, and social support, and how the measure of disease burden was developed and its purpose and use.

6. What are the variables for the study?

Example: This study uses two validated interview questionnaires to classify families on coping styles and social support. The Stress and Coping Scale (the SCDB-v2., cite) has two versions, one for adults with thirty items, and one for children with twelve items. The SCDB has been shown to reliably capture stress levels as one score, and the ways adults and children react to their stress as another score. The SCDB scoring methodology permits assignment of a coping style to each family member that characterizes the stress response as avoiding, monitoring, or motivating. The Carston Social Support Scale (CSSS, cite) provides information about the availability of and use of extended family or other support systems, such as schools, social services, and friends, in performing chores of daily living and stress relief.

I will use the Burden of Disease Rating Scale (BDRS, cite) from the health record to score the level of intensity of the disease as low, medium, and high. Key variables include family demographics, size of family, health status, income, and education.

7. Data Management

a. Methods of data collection

Example: The co-principal investigators (the research team) for this study project will conduct in-person interviews with families at the clinic by appointment. Privacy will be maintained as described in the IRB protocol. The scores for the BDRS will be obtained by the research team directly, by hand, from the electronic health record (EHR), recorded on a data collection form (approved by the IRB), and entered into the protected electronic study files. Demographic data will be collected from the EHR via a request to the Information Systems Department and transmitted as described in the IRB protocol. Other family descriptor variables will be collected in the interviews using the approved study data collection form.

b. Data entry, use, security

We will use [*specify the software*] for data entry and analysis. Include information about how the data from human subjects will be used and protected by security precautions.

c. Data analysis and interpretation strategies

Example: To answer the primary question of whether families differ in coping styles according to the disease burden score, we will use analysis of variance. To examine the secondary question of whether socioeconomic status, as a dichotomous variable, is associated with coping styles, we will use the discriminant analysis function of the software.

Because this is an exploratory study, we will also apply other descriptive and graphic display techniques to fully examine these data. For example, the social support factor may be a possible mediating factor between disease burden and stress scores.

Because this study may have a selection bias, we will compare the demographics, income levels, and disease burden scores of study subjects with the range and averages of these variables for the total population of families at the clinics.

8. Project Management Plan and Timelines

In this section, identify any project activities that need to be organized and structured to conduct the study.

In our example, families will be interviewed, so you should cover briefly the hours and locations for those events and who will conduct the interviews. Provide a simple timeline with the essential tasks. The timeline keeps you on track. The amount of detail depends on the complexity of your project. List the key steps and their start and ending dates by month or week according to your study schedule. For example, see the table below.

Activity	Month											
	1	2	3	4	5	6	7	8	9	10	11	12
Obtain IRB approval	X	X										
Complete literature review (if appropriate)				X								
Sample or case selection			X									
Subject enrollment				X	X	X	X					
Submit data requests				X								
Conduct surveys; Administer questionnaires						X	X	X				
Data collection				X	X	X	X	X				
Data entry and cleaning							X	X	X			
Analysis										X		
Results											X	
Study report or publications											X	X

9. Study Limitations

Example: This study is being conducted in three local family practice clinics, with first-come, first-enrolled families. This may result in a selection bias. The results may not be generalizable to a larger population. The measure of disease burden is a clinical decision algorithm and, therefore, is partially subjective.

10. Human Subjects

This project would require a full review by the governing Institutional Review Board as well as appropriate consent forms and protocols before it could begin.

11. Other Concerns, Issues, Considerations or Conditions for this Project

If there is anything unusual about your project, address it here. Examples might be holding a meeting with sixth grade teachers before you collect the reading comprehension scores to explain the study to them, or providing copies of human subject's approvals to the clinic operations manager before being allowed to acquire pre- and post-treatment scores, or getting authorization from the nursing department head at the hospitals where you will observe interactions between clients and nursing personnel.

Examples of introductions to the Structure & Methods section.

Example 1

As the evidence suggests, the Promotoras Community Education model has been successful in improving birth outcomes for women in poverty. The purpose of this study is to better understand what factors contribute to its success and summarize recommendations for improvements to the model. To accomplish this, I will conduct a focused review of the literature.

In the following paragraphs, I provide details of the process I will use for the literature search, the inclusion and exclusion criteria, the approach to analyzing the material, and the anticipated timeline for accomplishing this project.

Example 2

Because of the importance of community policing as part of community safety and access to psychiatric care, I will evaluate opinions of families of individuals with mental illness about their interactions with law enforcement. For this **cross-sectional survey research project**, *I will use the "Community Survey on Public Safety and Law Enforcement" from the U.S. Department of Justice Office of Community Oriented Policing Services (COPS Office). Surveys will be anonymous and voluntary.*

In the following paragraphs, I will first **describe the project methodology,** *then explain the variables I will use and how I will collect, manage, and analyze the data. Last, I have provided a timeline and milestones for completing the project.*

Example 3

The primary aim of this research project is to better understand whether diagnosis is related to frequency of admission to a psychiatric emergency center (the center). I will use a **retrospective case-control study design** *to compare admissions for a group of psychiatric outpatients with a dual diagnosis of a thought disorder and a substance abuse disorder with a group of thought disorder diagnosis patients with no substance abuse disorder. Thirty subjects* *in each group will be selected randomly from admissions to the center for calendar year 2003.* (Note, in an IRB proposal, you will explain specifically how you define "randomly.") ***Records will abstracted*** *for crisis services utilization for 12 months following the person's first admission to the center in 2003.*

EIGHT

Data Management

This chapter provides an orientation to data collection, data entry, and data analysis issues. You need a conversational knowledge of statistics for any scholarly project. I've provided some guidance on how to do this along with several sources for you to find trustworthy, basic information on statistical tests.

Data Collection (Template 11)

You have your list of variables and specifically how you have defined them. Now you want to collect those numbers or other information that will become the data set for your study.

Before you begin, you need to have the answers to ten minimally crucial questions. I've provided a list of questions in the table below. *Template 11* has more detailed items for you to complete.

When you are running through this checklist, remember that you should visualize your process and tasks. For example, if you need to collect information from a set of electronic health records, will you sit at a computer and search each record for one piece of data such as gender, and record it on another form, or will you write down all the information you need from each record before moving on to the next case?

In this century, one would think you might just query an electronic health record on your own. More likely, your institution or the research site has a central repository of data and a department to which you will submit a request. And, if you will submit a request for a set of data, in what format will you receive it? Will they let you specify the format, or will it be a coded data file that you will need to translate into another software platform?

Other considerations might include how the data points are defined in the electronic database. How are diagnoses coded? Are they date sensitive? Do you want the first diagnosis or the last? If it's a mental health study, how will the diagnoses be coded?

Ten Minimally Crucial Questions for Data Collection Planning

What data am I collecting or requesting?	Where are the data located?
Do I have authorized access?	Do I have to complete requests for data?
In what form or format do I want those data that I must request?	Do I have questionnaires or survey forms?
Are the DCFs or questionnaires in electronic or printed form?	If they are printed, how will I collect and store them? (You would have described this in the IRB protocol.)
Who will abstract data from electronic records or paper documents to a spreadsheet?	Will that spreadsheet be paper or electronic?

Data Collection Forms (DCFs)

DCFs are the tools you will use to record information, both quantitative and qualitative, that is both numbers and text. If you are conducting field research, your forms will differ from forms that record survey data, test data, or patient care data. Survey data should be entered twice. What? Yes, twice. This prevents error in data entry. Also, it is important to prevent fatigue when entering survey data or any data taken from a piece of paper to an electronic form. It is too easy for mistakes to occur in this type of process. The structure of the electronic form into which you will enter survey or questionnaire or test data must be created before you start data entry. Be sure to use both codes (numeric) and narrative text so you can decipher which variable is which. If you use standardized questionnaires or tests be sure to follow the instructions for constructing the data files. If there are computations involved, be sure your data is organized so that you can make those computations later. Always think ahead to any likely or unlikely problems that could arise before you enter data.

Let's assume you will use the following sources for your data.

- Electronic Health Record
- Paper or electronic source material such as questionnaires or tests previously collected
- Paper or electronic forms for collecting new information such as questionnaires (surveys) or tests
- Management databases such as billing, pharmacy, patient safety data, personnel records, or cost reports.

Your data should be organized by case. If necessary, use paper and pencil (not pen or ink) to record information so you can see it all spread out before your eyes. It is quite convenient actually to have a paper spreadsheet to use in meetings you may have about your project.

You may have several electronic data files depending on your study. You will want to combine them but only after each file is clean and organized. What does "cleaning" mean? It means ensuring that every field, every variable has the same style of information in a cell. Will you have numeric Codes for the International Classification of Diseases and a field for the name of the condition? How will you code missing data? Will you code no-response as missing?

Many software programs assist with cleaning data to unduplicate cases, correct fields such as date of birth and age, or identify fields with errors compared to the same type of field across cases. However, it remains the responsibility of the researcher to comb through the data with attention to details before attempting to perform analyses.

If possible, your DCFs should be organized the same way as the software you will use for data entry and analysis. For that reason, you should know what software layouts look like before you enter data. This will depend on your study design and the statistical tests you will use in your analysis. Most universities use either *IBM SPSS Statistics for Windows*, or SAS/ENGLISH™ software.

Generally speaking, the cases in these powerful analytic software programs are in rows, variables are in columns.

Always follow instructions for the analysis software if you have used a spreadsheet program to record your data, and you are attempting to import it.

Perhaps you only want to use a spreadsheet platform. Spreadsheet platforms are not statistical analysis platforms. However, you can use them for producing simple graphs and other visual representations of data.

Statistics

Statistics allow the content expert to get an answer to very specific questions. If you want a rational "nonmathematical" approach to grasping the statistics you will use for analyzing your data, refer to texts by Frost and by Motulsky in the references in Appendix 2.

"SOMETIMES IT DOES, SOMETIMES IT DOESN'T."

www.CartoonStock.com

Thus, for a research project that uses quantitative data, you need to interact with a biostatistician who is familiar with the health-related topic you will study. This person should effectively converse with and inform you within the context of your particular project. Not all scholarly projects or research studies use quantitative data.

If you are invested in your project, truly inspired by the study question, and have a compatible biostatistician, statistics for your project can be fun while still a bit mysterious.

Also, there are data analysis methods for descriptive studies that, while requiring no less intellectual investment, do not rely on traditional statistical hypotheses tests.

NINE

Specific Aims Section

Introduction

The Specific Aims section is the executive summary for your plan, and it is, therefore, at the front of the research plan. However, because it is a summary, and contains the research question and hypothesis, a statement of the value and importance of the study, and the way in which you will conduct all the necessary activities to complete it, I have addressed it last.

This is where you will state your study question, aim, goal, or hypothesis, and summarize the rationale and methods as an overall plan. For this reason, the Specific Aims does not come together as a whole until you have completed the Background & Importance <u>and</u> the Structure & Methods sections. Use *Template 12. Specific Aims* to complete this section with your material.

Specific Aims Content (Template 12)

1. Introduction

A normal human brain does not fully develop until young adulthood. Certain cognitive functions that may appear impaired in adolescents are actually simply not present. Questions persist about what determines if a youth goes to juvenile detention or to a psychiatric unit for treatment regardless of the precipitating behaviors.

2. The primary research aim and/or question

I propose to increase our understanding of the role cognitive functioning may have in the incarceration-treatment outcome for adolescent girls and boys in the local county institutions.

3. The null hypothesis (if it applies to your study)

My hypothesis is that there is no significant difference in cognitive functioning between the two groups. As a secondary question, I will evaluate the relationship between placement outcome and precipitating behavior.

4. A high-level statement of why you believe this project will add value to the field

Correctional systems and mental health systems tend not to share information about the adolescents in their care and custody. This prevents effective care coordination and may be an obstacle to achieving desirable health outcomes. If cognitive functioning does not differ between incarcerated and hospitalized youth, but precipitating behavior explains the placement, interventions for both groups could effectively include cognitive behavioral therapy.

5. Summary of the study structure and methods

Both systems collect and retain cognitive functioning test scores for the adolescent populations they serve. With appropriate approvals, I will use de-identified data for this study. Approximately fifty cases are available in each system. This number of subjects provides sufficient cases for [here use the information from your meeting with your statistics advisor about the statistical tests you will use, and how the sample size is sufficient]. There may be duplicate cases, in which situation, a secondary analysis of test score differences will be performed.

NOTE: A small sample size would increase the risk for a Type II error, meaning that you will have possibly missed detecting a difference or an effect where one truly exists.

I will use t-tests for the main hypothesis, and analysis of variance tests for sub-group analyses. Graphical displays such as scatterplots will add depth to the analysis process.

6. Write your concluding punch line

Better understanding the cognitive differences or similarities between incarcerated and hospitalized adolescents could change the way therapists apply cognitive therapy principles in each milieu.

JUNK DRAWER

"The applications are limitless."

TEN

Review of the Plan

Introduction and Overview

Now you have worked your way through each section of the plan. You know it is feasible, you have the necessary skills and abilities, your question or study aim is well defined, and you have the stage set for your project. You have the structure and approach mapped out, and you've summarized all the elements in the Specific Aims section as an executive summary.

As a recap, the study question launches the formal literature search and drives the structure or design and methods for the project. We covered the literature search in Chapter Five, because the source material you select from that search works for you across all sections of the plan.

Now you will assemble all the sections into one complete plan document. By developing each section in the order listed below, you have crystalized the scope of your project.

Assembling the Complete Plan (Template 13)

Template 13 is a fillable form where you can compile all the separate plan sections into one document. This is where you link the sections together seamlessly with connecting phrases.

There are ten pages in the template, with six components, and specific questions to help you construct one document:

1. The Study Question/Aim and Design/Structure
2. Literature, Background & Importance
3. Variables and Data Management
4. Structure & Methods
5. Human Subjects' Protection and Ethics
6. Scheduling Tasks

At right is an example of a table that you should create for your project with all the tasks you need to accomplish. You can also use this type of table to plan the project, keeping it as a master checklist as you develop the project plan. If you already have a format you prefer, use that format. As an option, I've provided this table in *Template 13*.

Task and Schedule Master Plan			
What – Tasks	**Date**	**Who**	**Result or Product**
Pre-study example: Power analysis	*Meet on Monday, January 15th*	*A biostatistician*	*Sample size*
Pre-study example: Complete DCFs	*Thursday, February 1*	*Me*	*Forms for IRB and for collecting data*
Request electronic health record data	*Monday, March 15th*	*Me and Info Systems contact*	*Clear expectations on data acquisition*
Example: Final interpretation of findings	*Tuesday, May 20th*	*Me, Advisor, Statistician*	*Draft findings, data visualizations*
Example: Submit final report/produce poster	*Tuesday, June 6*	*Me, Advisor, Statistician, Research Office contact*	*Report or Poster*

ELEVEN

Other Project Structures

Introduction

In this chapter, I've covered five types of research or scholarly projects that may not comport with the traditional designs. These include:

- Case Study
- Focused Review of the Literature
- Survey Research
- Exploratory and Developmental Studies
- Field Research and Observational Studies

Case Study

One individual or multiple cases of a rare condition or observation. Not a sample.

A case study is not a *case-control* study. This type of project structure is used to better understand a rare or complex phenomenon in depth. It can be used to describe a new procedure or a complex diagnosis. It can be used to explore challenges in diagnostic processes.

A case study project can use more than one case with the same condition or phenomenon. It may be feasible to extrapolate or pull and pool information and data or statistics from several case studies to make observations that might yield insights otherwise not revealed in one case study. Be creative!

Healthcare professionals have ample opportunities to experience rare or complex cases and analyze several as observational studies under one phenomenological umbrella. For example, nursing students may be interested in describing cases of teenage patients who do and don't recover from intensive care following car accidents in which they were driving. It is the story told by the case details that contribute to our understanding of recovery in this situation.

Each professional group has websites and literature that would guide you in a feasible and meaningful direction if you choose this strategy.

Focused Review of the Literature

In 2012, the *Journal of Primary Care & Community Health* published a study four colleagues and I submitted that was a focused review of the literature. We didn't call it *a focused review*, we titled it "Evidence-Based Guidance for Culturally Sensitive Assessment and Interventions for Perinatal Depression in Black American Women: A Synthesis of Published Research, 2008–2011" *https://pubmed.ncbi.nlm.nih.gov/23804173/*.

The question we were addressing was whether there was enough evidence-based research to inform primary care providers, in one paper, how to be more sensitive to cultural and racial factors when evaluating depressive symptoms in women during and after pregnancy.

This illustrates the opportunity to ask a question for this type of research, such as what do we know in a comprehensive way about race and low-birth-weight infants? This is different from a broad review of literature on a selected topic to prepare to conduct a research study.

This type of project can provide insights into topics in healthcare that have not been coalesced into meaningful interpretive prose. For example, there is a plethora of research on low-birth-weight infants, from perinatal factors to access to care to socioeconomic factors, but no one has combed through the literature to determine if there are any findings that would shed light on a particular population such as women under age 20 or 25, or teenage girls.

A focused review is not a meta-analysis, but it does require a large number of journal articles that you would catalog and abstract their data and statistics so you can evaluate the material and make cogent observations. Those observations would be backed up in such a way as to ask important future research questions or posit a missed opportunity in healthcare policies. You won't worry about attrition among your subjects, or defining your variables, unless you find too many articles with too many different measures. The published research you use needs to be coherent, similar in most ways to each other.

A note about systematic reviews and meta-analyses. A systematic review of the literature is another type of project, guidelines for which may be found in the following journal article and in the references list at the end of that article: BMJ 2009, 339:b2700 doi: _https://doi.org/10.1136/bmj.b2700_.

When you get into this realm, there are specific criteria and guidelines to follow, and decisions about how to treat data abstraction and synthesis.

A meta-analysis is a quantitative, structured, formal, epidemiological study design using sophisticated techniques to draw conclusions about a preponderance of evidence amassed from large experimental research studies. If you have an advisor who conducts meta-analysis studies, and you are interested in this statistical strategy, read their published papers and discuss them with that person.

Survey Research

A survey is a questionnaire that collects information about a subject using a distribution method such as e-mail, through a website, or in-person interviews. If you want to use a survey to collect data, define your primary question with great care, consult a reputable text on survey construction, and pilot test it before starting your project.

You could use a survey in a correlational, cross-sectional, or cohort study design. Survey data may be part of a larger study or a focus by itself. A survey can be used in an exploratory, developmental research project to contribute to our knowledge on the subject/s of interest.

You can conduct a survey with a group. For example, you can distribute a survey at a clinic and provide a box for deposit of the completed survey. Mail surveys can be inexpensive but labor intensive. You should always include a pre-paid return envelope. You will need to get consent procedures approved by an IRB.

You can conduct a personal one-on-one interview, which is time consuming but also inexpensive. You can use the telephone for this or recruit subjects —you can purchase lists of names and addresses.

Online questionnaires are more efficient, and your institution may provide resources to assist with that through your research mentor.

Collected responses are coded to analyze with appropriate statistical tests.

Limitations: Response rates are decidedly low for questionnaires not taken in person, and even with in-person administration, responses to some items may be low. The questionnaire has to be understandable to the target population. Readability is a sine-qua-non, so you must pre-test any questionnaire on a group representative of the population of interest.

Selecting and Designing Questionnaires

When conducting a study using a questionnaire to measure a condition or outcome, consider existing instruments. It is better to use an existing instrument in a novel way—with a new population, for example—than to develop your own questionnaire.

You can modify an existing survey, but not an instrument used to detect symptoms or diagnose a condition. You must describe how and why you are modifying it because you will lose its validity and reliability qualities.

If you are recording information never collected, consult with someone who knows how to construct interview questionnaires. Your mentor should be able to direct you if you are in this area of research protocols.

Seek out expert advice and guidance. There are multiple sources of information on designing valid and reliable questionnaires. Sampling is of critical importance and bias is another concern in the design and use of questionnaires.

Exploratory and Developmental

Exploratory and developmental studies examine existing information to better understand an observed phenomenon.

Characterizing Study Design

In 2014, a graduate student in geography published a paper she described as a "quantitative study" of education in one U.S. state. You can find the paper at *http://mds.marshall.edu/etd*, along with numerous other papers by students at Marshall University. I refer you to that paper because the study can be characterized in several different ways. First, it is a study of factors that were hypothesized, based on the available literature and other source material, to be associated with education attainment in the state of interest, with a focus on bachelor's degree attainment, and is thus a correlational study. Second, it could be considered a cross-sectional study using a convenience sample, collecting data from multiple state and national repositories. Third, the student used choropleth-mapping and other geo-coding techniques that underscore how visual data representations enrich the descriptive power of this kind of study. The paper places the state of interest in context to surrounding states and all states, demonstrating the value of comparisons. The conclusions for the paper reach beyond the original study aims, further enriching the findings and generating new questions that could inspire additional research.

Mixed-Methods

A 2017 paper in an Austrian journal (*Kolner Z Soz Sozpsychol*. 2017; 69 (Suppl 2): 107–131. Published online 2017 Jul 5. doi:*10.1007/s11577-017-0454-1*) provides details on how to design a mixed-methods study. In that paper, the authors suggest that the strategy of using mixed-methods (i.e., a variety of quantitative and qualitative methods) expands the opportunities for insights into the topic being studied and nuances in the data. This paper, and others both cited and similar, is a scholarly work that comes close to analyzing analyses strategies.

A mixed-method design is purposeful, not accidental. Collecting both quantitative and qualitative information for a study or using several different analytic techniques in a study does not make it a mixed-methods design. Within the mixed-method approach to research there are several sub-types of designs. Generally speaking, a mixed-method approach would apply more appropriately to experimental research or to field research, or observational studies. This type of project would be large in scope and typically involve a lengthy period of engagement with a cohort.

Field Research and Observational Studies

This type of research is for theory building, for understanding a little-understood or rare or rarely studied events or phenomenon. Protocols, and adherence to them, are crucial to quality field research. Protocols include, for example, how one regulates consistency in who does the observations, how and in what form observations are recorded, what specific elements are attended to in the course of observing and recording the information, and the timing, intrusion factors, and environmental factors.

Information collected in field or observational studies is usually analyzed with qualitative methods such as organizing, classifying, examining trends and pattern, or content analysis techniques.

Methods of data collection vary, such as using video or photography, illustrations, audio recordings or logs.

Because this method is sensitive to the observer and the subjects or activities being observed, skills and abilities need to be developed and practiced before venturing into this type of study.

Here are some example ideas for field or observational studies in healthcare.

Observe psychology assessments in a trauma unit: Become part of the team when they make rounds in a trauma unit. Record the process of collecting and recording patient information. Does it differ based on the status of the patient, or their injuries, or the time of the day, or the composition of the assessment team?

Observe interactions in case conferences: Become a scribe for case conferences. Record and analyze the different types and characteristics of the cases reviewed, participants in the process, amount of time spent on each case, and the results. Look for patterns based on case complexity or participants to the conference for example.

Observe several nursing stations in one or more hospitals: Research patterns of activities and interactions at a variety of units, such as a pediatric unit, a post-op cardiac unit, and a neo-natal intensive care unit. Select the same shift for all observations. Document, then compare, the number of encounters, the purpose of each, the outcomes of each, and the after-encounter actions at the station (discussing it, follow-up activities, or accompanying the party to the encounter). Look for patterns that distinguish or connect the different units.

TWELVE

Scientific Writing

In this chapter, you will find tips and guidance on preparing your finding, writing well, and why manuscripts are rejected.

Good Writing Habits and Tips

Parsimony is essential and expected in scientific narratives. Parsimonious means that you are frugal with your words. Use the simplest assumptions for theories or interpreting data. "Occam's razor" is sometimes called the principle of parsimony.

These days it is usually interpreted to mean something like "the simpler the explanation, the better" or "don't multiply hypotheses unnecessarily." Select cautiously from among theories with equal explanatory power, and when giving explanatory reasons for something, avoid positing more than is necessary.

Some tips for writing the narrative sections of your plan.

- Use a single space rather than double spaces between a period and the beginning of a sentence.
- Use tables or columns instead of lengthy vertical lists of items.
- Limit excessive use of modifiers.

- Use active voice.
- Choose words carefully. Be selective and expressive but factual—don't editorialize.
- Keep it simple and logical.
- Use "this study" or "this proposed study" in reference to your project. Use "that study" or "their study" to reference another person's work.
- Don't use the term "etc." Be precise. If there is too much to list in a sentence, use a table. On occasion you can say "such as" or "including but not limited to."
- Use the terms "valid" and "reliable" wisely. There are many different types of validity and reliability. Refer to a glossary of research terms. Ensure you are correctly using these and other research terms.
- A finding is either significant or not significant. Some authors erroneously use modifiers such as "highly" or "greatly." This is not sound research language.
- Pay close attention to noting the p-values from hypothesis testing to support the strength of evidence to reject the null hypothesis, and confidence intervals for effect sizes.
- Always use correct grammar. Check and have others check your spelling. Do not rely solely on the computer for spelling or grammar checks.
- The phrase "account for" means that one variable explains a portion of the observed effects. For example, "age" may account for a portion of the difference between the time men and women take to fall asleep.
- You may use first person.
- Get at least two detail-oriented individuals to read the plan for you.

Reasons for Manuscript and Proposal Rejections

There are published articles about writing manuscripts properly and the most common reasons why they, and proposals, are rejected. Research Medics' website offers writing and editing services. **Marisa Granados, Research Medics Editorial Desk, has written an article "Top Ten Reasons Papers Get Rejected," April 11, 2018. Her article can be found at**: _https://researchmedics.com/top-ten-reasons-papers-get-rejected/_. Here are a few of the reasons she addresses.

- Errors or omissions in citing landmark studies
- Incoherent or unsupported project rationale
- Inappropriate study design
- Writing conclusions unsupported by the data and the analysis

— THIRTEEN —

Human Subjects' Protections and the IRB

There is a clear difference and distinction between a research proposal or plan, and a proposal to an Institutional Review Board (the IRB, or any other name your institution uses for this function). The IRB proposal, sometimes referred to as the Protocol Synopsis, will include parts of your plan that you can copy and paste into an IRB form. You may also append your project plan to an IRB proposal if your institution permits it.

Be cautious and be informed about this. You should assume that any study using information from or about an individual (referred to as a human subject) requires IRB approval that includes the method for protecting that information. In some cases, research will require something called a "HIPAA" waiver that protects you and the subject from having private (personal) health information shared without permission and in case of error or mistakes. HIPAA refers to the Health Insurance Portability and Accountability Act of 1996.

In this chapter, I've provided only general guidance on this critical section of your project plan because every institution has, or is affiliated with an organization that has, rules and regulations and procedures governing human subjects in research. Boards or committees that govern the conduct of human subjects' research are known by various names. The most common is the Institutional Review Board (IRB), but other names may include ethics or ethical review board, or research ethics committee.

The Health and Human Services agency at the federal government level has an Office for Human Research Protections (OHRP). Its website is: *https://www.hhs.gov/ohrp/*. The OHRP issues rules and regulations and specifies protected or special populations by gender, age, race and ethnicity, and other criteria such as incarcerated individuals, or prisoners. If you use the OHRP website for any reason, be aware that many rules and regulations govern clinical or experimental research. Use your analytic thinking skills to sort through the information most relevant to your study design or project structure.

The IRB's purpose is to safeguard information about individuals and to protect research subjects from harm. The review process ensures that a person who consents to participate or allow their information to be used in a study is treated fairly, and protects the institutions where the researcher works as well as where the research is conducted. An IRB ensures that prevailing ethical and legal practices are followed. The IRB also serves the purpose of assuring the federal government, and other granting agencies, as appropriate, that grant applications for federal funding have been reviewed according to all applicable rules and regulations. You must have approval from the authority that governs human subjects' research before you begin any part of your project.

The IRB protocol or proposal you submit focuses on multiple aspects of a project involving the collection, analysis, storage, and reporting of information from and about humans. That information is referred to as Protected Health Information, or PHI. You may also see the term PII, or Personal Identifying Information.

There are several different types of IRB review, including exempt, expedited, full board, and continuing. Also, there are procedures for protocol amendments or modifications. Note that "exempt" does not mean exempt from review—it means exempt from full board review. The determination of the type of review is based on the risk to the study subject. Risk is broadly defined. The IRB website at your institution should have plenty of details for you to consider as you begin this leg of your journey.

In your plan, you will have described your study subjects or their data and how you will draw the sample based on inclusion/exclusion criteria. In the IRB proposal, you will also need to explain why you use those inclusion/exclusion criteria. If your study is about perinatal depression, you will, as odd as it may seem, state why you excluded male subjects.

In the IRB protocol, you will address in detail any activities associated with data: how study data are collected or acquired, where and under what circumstances, who has access to those data, how those data are secured to prevent unauthorized access or loss, how long data and data collection forms are kept, and how you dispose of study data.

Only under certain conditions can you use protected (personal) health information (PHI) from an individual (study subject) without permission and/or complicated consent procedures and documents. If you are using existing data, you may need to have a certificate of confidentiality (which may go by other names).

The rules on using information that may be used to identify an individual in a research study govern all study designs and structures, with the possible exception of a case study.

Alternatively, you can use public domain or public use data or data that has no PHI by signing an appropriate agreement with the source agent.

Minimal information in this section includes:

- Description of the study population
- Rationale for including one population and excluding another (inclusion and exclusion criteria)

- Attention given to defined special populations
- Risks, both known and unknown, to study participants
- Safeguards against foreseen and unforeseen risks
- Potential benefits of the research to the study subjects and to others
- Importance of the knowledge to be gained

Write your Human Subjects' Protection section using your applicable IRB guidelines. Be specific, thorough, perhaps overly thorough, and comprehensive. A delay in an IRB approval process can interfere with the timelines for your project.

Terminology, Study Designs & Project Structures

1. Research Concepts and Terminology

This appendix provides definitions for the most common terminology you will encounter as you construct a research project, conduct its associated activities, and read and write about research.

The concepts for which I have provided brief definitions **are not in alphabetical order.** I find that when these concepts are alpha-ordered, the relationships between and among them may be lost to the reader, thus confusing. **Instead, I have grouped these concepts according to their relationships.**

This is not a statistics manual; thus many statistical terms are only briefly described, and recommendations are provided to seek additional information in statistics texts. Because this Research Project Planning Guide is not a book about statistics, it is important to refer to reliable texts to ensure clarity in your selection and use of variables. You may hear many different terms tossed about in discussions about "data."

I recommend referring to *Introduction to Statistics: An Intuitive Guide for Analyzing Data and Unlocking Discoveries* by J. Frost, *https://statisticsbyjim.com/.*

Observed Phenomenon

An observed phenomenon is a term used to denote an event, condition, or situation that you see or learn of that can be speculated about, studied, explained, or better understood.

Research or Study Question

For non-experimental research, the question is a posited situation or set of conditions that can be studied or explored by collecting and analyzing relevant information to discover, reveal, deduce, or speculate on a conclusion or observation. It is a wondering that elicits speculation. It does not call for any action to test, modify, or manipulate any person, animal, condition, or object.

Hypothesis

Merriam-Webster defines hypothesis as an assumption or concession made for the sake of argument, defining a condition capable of being verified or disproved by observation or experiment.

Null Hypothesis

Inherent in the study hypothesis (e.g., sixth grade classes with a teacher–student ratio of less than 1:40 perform better on reading comprehension tests than those with more students per teacher) is the possibility that there is no difference in performance between classes defined thusly. That is a null hypothesis: a statement that there is no effect of a variable on a population/outcome, or no difference in effect between two or more groups. It is the condition you are trying to demonstrate is not true, to disprove or "reject."

Study Design
Study design is the framework that will guide your data collection and analysis. You select it based on your question, your hypothesis, and the types of data you will use.

Variable
A variable is a construct of interest that has a measurable trait or characteristic that may exist in differing amounts or types and may change, predict, or be related to other variables in a study.

The nature of a variable may be referred to the same way one refers to the nature of data (i.e., nominal, ordinal, continuous, interval, or ratio). According to the role of a variable in a study, it may be considered to be dependent or independent, predictor, or correlated. A variable is cast according to the study structure and question, and as suits the statistical analysis approach.

If you're shopping for dinner and you want a salad, there are many variables that might determine the kind of salad you have. Green leafy vegetables are one variable. Your choice of one may suggest the rest of the ingredients, depending on its characteristics and assuming the types can be identified and labeled. This is similar to the idea that age may be associated with preference for the color of a new car.

Blood pressure is a variable. Data define variables. Data defining blood pressure are systolic and diastolic pressure numbers. In this example, blood pressure may be an "outcome" variable, if its values are hypothesized to be the result of an intervention, or if a health condition or event is suspected to be related to them.

Outcome Variable
The word "outcome" connotes a result or consequence of an action, as in *health outcomes are the result of treatments*. For experimental research, it is the variable that a researcher speculates will change or be affected by other conditions or an intervention. For non-experimental

research, an outcome variable would be the condition you are interested in as the one you think will change or vary or differ according to changes in other study variables, not an intervention intended to affect it.

In this book, I often use the term "variable of interest" to designate the condition, event, or quality that is of primary interest in your study question.

You will hear the term "outcome variable" frequently used in health research.

Let's explore the concept. If I use a case-control design, comparing the conditions to which a group of children with measles and one without measles were exposed, and I include the variables of day-care status, in-home babysitters, school age siblings, and visitors to the home, the outcome of interest is still measles, and the other conditions are predictor or correlated variables.

If I study the relationship between parenting style and disease burden, there is no outcome variable, and no truly dependent or independent variable, because there is no expectation that one influences, changes, or predicts the occurrence of another.

If I use a cross-sectional design and study whether sixth grade students in classrooms with high student–teacher ratios have lower scores in reading comprehension than students in classrooms with low student–teacher ratios, test scores could be considered an outcome variable, but a relationship between the two variables of interest would not mean that the student–teacher ratio *caused* the observed scores.

Methods

Methods are the tools and processes or procedures you will use in conducting your project. Methods include at least the definition of variables and the data you will collect to measure them; selection of cases or participants; data collection tools, tasks, and management; and the statistical analysis, findings, and interpretation strategies.

Data

Data is plural. Datum is singular. That's your Latin lesson for today. Always say "data are," never say "data is," even though others may. Data are used to describe, define, or characterize variables.

Statistics

Merriam-Webster defines statistics as the branch of mathematics dealing with the collection, analysis, interpretation, and presentation of masses of numerical data; a collection of quantitative data.

NOTE: Statistics guides abound, on the internet and in book vendors. Some are in plain language (as plain as you can get in statistics!) and extremely helpful for a sense of direction. No matter what project you are doing, some statistics or data analysis software and methods will be involved. Cultivate a meaningful relationship with a biostatistician who understands your field and will work with you and inspire and guide you, not merely direct you.

Statistical Tests

A statistical test is a tool, method, or formula for determining if there is enough evidence in the data to reject the null hypothesis and provide other information about the variables such as mean, median, confidence intervals, or coefficients.

Findings

Findings are what you discover from the research project. It is the results of your study. Findings include test statistics and interpretation of the results, an explanation or discussion of what you found or observed, any speculation you have about why your study had a particular outcome, and questions raised by the results.

Effect

Effect, or effect size, is statistical term used to quantify the difference between two groups. It is an interpretation of a difference that puts it into context. Statistical analysis is based on formulae that fit assumptions about the shape and type of data under analysis. Effect sizes are classified differently according to the question and study structure. There are alternative statistics that can be used. Consult a statistics text for more information.

P-value

The P-value is the probability of obtaining the same or larger effect observed in your sample if you assume the null hypothesis is true. $P = 0.1$ can be interpreted as a 1% chance that you'd observe your sample effect or more extreme if the null hypothesis is correct.

Statistical Significance

If you use statistical tests to determine if your study has detected a difference or an effect that is strong enough to reject the null hypothesis, you'll be dealing with a significance level. If a test result provides a statistic with a significance "level" of .01, your results are significant at the .01 level, meaning there is a 1 in 100 chance of it being incorrect.

Errors (in hypothesis testing)

The most common use of the term "error" applies to statistical hypothesis testing. This is one of the terms you should be conversant with if you are going to analyze data with statistical tests.

The two kinds of error associated with hypothesis testing are Type I (one) and Type II (two).

Type I means the researcher rejected the null hypothesis when it was true. The researcher identified false positive results.

Type II means the researcher supported the null hypothesis when it was not true. In other words, the researcher missed identifying a difference or effect when it actually was present.

You can easily find many different tables that illustrate what these types of errors mean. A table might help you understand the balance between Type I and Type II errors that a study structure should pursue.

Errors may also be associated with other aspects of research.

One other familiar way the term error appears in research is in reference to "the standard error" of a statistic. In this situation, it refers to a characteristic of a study sample compared to the whole population.

Validity

Validity as a concept has several applications.

"Is the study valid?" This is a reference to an assessment of the overall structural integrity and accuracy of a study. It applies to the design and to the methods of research, and their suitability for answering the study question or testing the research hypothesis.

A valid study has no fatal flaws, but it may have limitations. Limitations may be related to availability of data, size of the sample population in the study, or other factors. The researcher always declares the limitations of a study. A valid study uses a design that provides the correct vehicle to answer the research question or test the hypothesis.

Ideally, all variables known to be associated with a given condition would be included. If you cannot accurately and fully measure what you say you will measure, you should re-think the project.

For a small study, you should be concerned about being able to support and back up with evidence, the rationale, and all the elements of your plan as being true, accurate, and appropriate for your study.

To be sure you are constructing a valid study, search the published literature or facts about the condition of interest.

"Is this questionnaire valid?" A valid instrument is one that accurately captures data about the variable—it measures what it purports to measure. To be sure of this, you would consider studies similar to yours using the same tools you propose to use.

Validity is quantified and discussed in user manuals or in published findings from studies of face, content, construct, and other types of validity for specific instruments.

If the study is about factors contributing to length of stay in a psychiatric hospital, it would not include information about patients who have never had a psychiatric hospital stay.

A study of academic achievement among grade school children with food insecurities in single-parent households won't include high school age youth or children in a two-parent home.

A study of the influence of staff attitudes on an outcome of interest should use a questionnaire with evidence that it includes factors contained in the study's definition of attitudes.

A questionnaire about recovery expectations for persons with drug dependencies would be developed and tested using a range of value constructs reported as associated with recovery.

Reliability

Reliability is an assessment of the consistency of a measure over time. Be careful, because it is possible to measure something consistently over time while not measuring it accurately. A measurement may be valid and unreliable, or reliable but not valid. Information about measurement tool reliability will be in a user manual or in the literature.

Sensitivity and Specificity

These terms are statistics used in evidence-based science to communicate the ability of a test to correctly identify individuals with (true positive) and without (true negative) a given condition. If you want to include these constructs in your study, you should have achieved competence in using them, or you should seek additional information and training.

Generalize

This statistics-based term—and its sister, generalizability—relates to whether the results of a study apply to a larger population than the groups in that study. You can read more about generalizing from qualitative or non-experimental studies in the research literature.

Bias

The term bias refers to any deviation from accuracy in all aspects of study design, implementation, and reporting. In statistics, biased results are not accurate results—not reliable or trustworthy. Bias may occur intentionally (this is not dishonesty) or unintentionally in many aspects of conducting research. For example, it may appear in the definition of variables, the method of selecting subjects or cases (sample), the choice of data sources, and in collecting, analyzing, interpreting, and reporting data. Study limitations must be identified and discussed to fully explain any unintentional risk for bias in the research.

Institutional Review Board (IRB)

An IRB is a formal group of experts who review, provide guidance, and give or withhold permission for conduct of a research study using humans as participants and/or using Protected Health Information (PHI). An IRB, under any institutional name, follows established international guidelines as well as national and local rules and regulations on research with human subjects.

2. Research Designs and Project Structures

Case-Control Study

A case-control study design is used when you want to explain why some people develop a certain condition while others do not. You would need a group of people with a specified condition, such as diabetes (Cases), and a matched group (Controls) without the condition. The purpose is to learn whether one group with diabetes was exposed to different factors than another group without the condition. This is how health-screening tools are developed.

An example of a question using this design would be: Why do some nulliparous women (in a specific age range, of specific racial and/or ethnic origins) develop post-partum depression, and another group with similar characteristics does not?

Generally, you would use this design to gain insights into rare or little-understood conditions. These insights can provide valuable information for public health, treatment protocols, prevention strategies, and environmental concerns.

Why? A case-control study determines, through the use of statistics called "odds ratios" and "confidence intervals" using probability theory, whether persons with the condition were at greater risk (i.e., had more exposure/factors than those who did not develop the condition). If this is not the case, and there is not a statistically significant difference between the groups, there must be other unknown factors contributing to its presence.

This design begins with the outcome of interest. First, you identify the condition of interest and use historical data to compare the extent to which Group A and Group B were exposed to factors known to contribute to its existence.

Benefit? A case-control study helps learn more about what might be done to prevent the condition under study. You could also use it to understand how to *create or introduce a condition that you want someone to have or acquire.*

This study design is best suited to gain insights into rare or little-understood conditions. These insights can provide valuable information for public health, treatment protocols, prevention strategies, and environmental concerns.

Case-Control: Examples and Discussion

Two groups of patients with the same diagnosis, one group has a history of admission to a crisis unit, another has never been admitted. *The condition of interest is the admission status for persons with bipolar disorder.* You would select the two groups on matching variables such as gender, age, length of time with the disease, social support structure, and medication. You could further refine the condition of interest to include only to only first admission patients. You might discover that never-admitted patients are at risk for being admitted, or have better social support structures.

Two groups of post-hip surgery women over age 50, one with weight gain, the other with stable weights. *The condition of interest is weight gain.*

You would develop a list of suspected factors such as high carbohydrate diet, amount or frequency of exercise, time spent in rehabilitation, and quality of life. You would select two groups of post-surgery women over age 50, one with (case – condition) and one without (control – no condition) weight gain, established as a weight threshold.

Two groups of children in the same grade in a specific school, one with grades above a specified cut-off level in all classes, and one below that cut-off score. Do these groups differ? Variables might include age, gender, race, ethnicity, IQ score, family size, and income (if you couldn't get income, use a proxy such as qualified/not qualified for low-income programs), same-school siblings (yes/no), and the presence or absence of medical conditions.

Case-Control: Cautions

Before proceeding with this design, consult a biostatistician on the sample size needed to calculate odds ratios. If you cannot obtain sufficient cases to satisfy your desired precision, consider the relative value of the study topic, consider modifying your definitions to narrow the focus, or select a different but suitable design for your study.

In designing a case-control study, you must be rigorous in defining the condition and matching the groups to protect against bias or errors.

Cohort Design

A cohort is a group of individuals studied over time. A cohort study compares a condition in one group at a baseline measurement, to an endpoint measurement. It is usually prospective.

You may also have a retrospective cohort that begins years or X time ago and has an endpoint closer to the present time, similarly to a case-control study but with one group.

You can study two groups or sub-groups matched on specific characteristic/s (gender, age, diagnosis, exposure, or possessing some other characteristic such as a common experience).

A cohort study may require a long period of time such as a year, unless there is a short-acting event that occurred, the effects of which you want to measure. For prospective studies there is a risk of losing study subjects unless there is an incentive/compensation for time and travel.

A cohort study is exploratory and developmental and may lead larger research and theory building. It can provide insight to risk factors and may explain how to achieve desired clinical outcomes in specific groups.

Cross-Sectional Design

A cross-sectional design aims to describe a population on selected variables. Cross-sectional is a concept that applies to the way the sample of the population is drawn.

Use this design to study a set of factors in a specified slice of time. In a cross-sectional design the researcher typically uses existing data or a sample of subjects in a particular setting and takes one measurement to describe a condition at a given point in time.

This type of design can be used for research questions that are not driven by a hypothesis, but targets a lesser understood phenomenon. Use this design to estimate the prevalence of a condition of interest in a population. This cross-sectional structure can be used to generate questions for further study, or to improve our understanding of a condition's prevalence.

You may have a clinic that began using cognitive behavioral therapy last year and you want to use a sample of female patients between the ages of 25 and 35, with specific diagnoses, to describe changes in pre and post testing scores the therapist recorded. Or you might study the records of a group of adolescents in a juvenile justice detention center, with charges of family violence, to describe factors associated with the case disposition. Those factors of interest might include the number and type of previous charges, any previous convictions, the presence of legal counsel, and standard demographics. Your question might be: Are case dispositions for adolescents charged with family violence, related to the presence or absence of legal counsel? Your results may find difference between age groups, but the primary question is an overall one.

If there are adequate numbers to power a study, exploratory data analysis tools will enable you to provide a rich descriptive narrative and graphic representations.

Correlational Study

A correlational design is used to examine or explore relationships between selected characteristics, qualities, or conditions within one group.

The word correlational means co-related. If a condition such as age is related to another condition such as income, it would be co-related. It may be co-related positively or negatively. As one changes, the other changes also. You can ask whether gender is related to color preference, or you may use continuous data to ask whether scores on a test are related to hours of sleep.

Correlational studies can utilize existing data. If your mentor has a large data set from an experimental research study, you might be permitted to explore a subset of those data.

Use this design if you think a condition changes in relationship to change in another condition. For example, do you think that as age increases, income increases? Is age related to recovery time from knee injuries? Is quality of life related to profession?

With this design for a project, you can study two variables, or use a more complex factorial design with multiple variables. In this study design, the statistical tests look for direction and strength of relationships between variables. Correlation results help generate questions for future research, generate theories, develop models for testing, and are relatively easy to manage.

Analyses of these data are intriguing because you can use visual graphics such as scatter plots to look at the shape of the data. One useful example is The Circumplex Model of Marital and Family Systems (CMMFS; Olson, Sprenkle, & Russell, 1979), in which both linear and curvilinear relationships can be found.

Correlational Design: Cautions

This type of design can quickly become large in size and broad in scope. It can also lead to spurious results if you have omitted factors known to be associated with the condition, or you have included variables not considered reasonably or logically likely to be associated with the condition.

If knowledge in your topic of interest is limited, and no published studies have identified relationships among the variables you wish to explore, it will be easier to explore your interests with less worry about omitting an important variable.

This type of design is useful to formulate additional questions or hypothesis about a phenomenon. Never underestimate the power of making a contribution to science.

Correlational Design: Examples and Discussion

Is a history of jail incarceration associated with frequency of admission to a psychiatric crisis unit? Population would be patients admitted to a crisis unit.

Notice this does not say "is jail incarceration associated," but instead, says "is a history of incarceration associated." History implies more than frequency. It implies context. In this case, the variables would include at least the number of crisis unit admissions in a specified time frame, number of previous times in jail, arrest charges classified as violent and nonviolent, or more specific such as drug possession, burglary, assault, and diagnoses, preferably on all axis (for data prior to DSM-V).

Is race or age more strongly associated with post-partum depression?

Population would be a multi-racial, multi-ethnic group of women who have given birth, diagnosed with post-partum depression. You would include age, race, and ethnicity, and a measure of depression using data collected with a standardized scale. Your question is about race and age, but you could include the number of children at home, single-parent household status, income, and other variables that might also be related to a woman developing post-partum depression.

Is childhood trauma associated with self-esteem scores in women between the ages of 21 and 35 diagnosed with major depressive disorder (MDD)?

Population would be women in the age group of interest with a documented diagnosis of MDD. Define the measures used for childhood trauma and self-esteem, and take a cross-sectional sample at local mental health centers. This would be a correlational study.

Potential for a different design

Could that question about MDD, trauma history, and self-esteem be studied using a case-control design? Yes, if you are doing a retrospective assessment of risk factors for MDD. However, the question above speculates on a relationship between trauma histories and self-esteem. You might have a group of 30 women who were victims of violence as children, or other traumatic experiences according to your interest, and a group who report they have not been exposed to specific traumatic events. Both groups would have a diagnosis of MDD. For a case-control study of this topic, there may be other factors to explore in a case-control study such as history of incarceration, education, and such.

Correlational studies can utilize existing data. If your mentor has a large data set from an experimental research study, you might be permitted to explore a subset of those data. Correlation results help generate questions for future research, generate theories, develop models for testing, and are relatively easy to manage.

Analyses of these data are intriguing because you can use visual graphics such as scatter plots to look at the shape of the data points. One example is The Circumplex Model of Marital and Family Systems (CMMFS; Olson, Sprenkle, & Russell, 1979) in which both linear and curvilinear relationships can be found.

Case Study

A case study is not a *case-control* study. This type of research might be suitable if your aim is to better understand a rare or complex phenomenon.

A case study project can be more rewarding and productive if you can have more than one case. It is feasible to combine information and data or statistics from several studies into observations that might yield insights otherwise not revealed in one case study. Be creative!

Health professional students most likely to benefit from this type of study include nursing, psychology, social work, and alternative medicine such as homeopathy, naturopathic, or holistic. In medicine, there are ample opportunities to identify rare or complex cases and analyze several as observational studies under one phenomenological umbrella.

Each professional group has websites and literature that would guide you in a feasible and meaningful direction if you choose this strategy.

Focused Review of the Literature

A focused review of the literature in your topic of interest is not a "study design" per se, but it is an important option for a scholarly project. This is not a meta-analysis, so you would not use data or statistical tests. You would not be concerned about having enough cases or subjects to ensure validity. This type of project structure is for studies that aim to redirect, or guide policies and practices by amassing substantial quantities of information from published research that has not been analyzed for trends, or for indicators of population differences that have not been studied independently.

Survey Research

This is not a *design* per se, but it is sometimes thought of that way. A survey is really a research tool; a method of collecting information. Even so, you'll see books that use this term as if it were its own "design." Survey research is used for understanding consumer opinions or behaviors in the commercial realm, but also in social work, psychology, and education.

Exploratory & Developmental

Exploratory and Developmental Studies examine existing information to better understand an observed phenomenon. This is typically used to learn more about a little-studied population or event or phenomenon. It generates information and questions that can lead to additional research.

Field or Observational Studies

Similarly to other types of research, a field or observational study extrapolates or draws inferences from a sample population to the relevant general population. Case studies, cross-sectional studies, and longitudinal or cohort study designs may incorporate observation as a method for collecting data. This type of study is meant for real world information gathering, collecting observations of people or animals in natural or contrived conditions that are not experimental. In healthcare research guidelines may be applicable to meet criteria that guards against errors in this type of research.

3. Research Designs and Project Structures with Example Questions and Aims

Cross-Sectional Study

What is the prevalence of children with developmental disabilities among women in extreme poverty? Measure a sample from five years of existing and new births.
For first responders, in the year following the attacks of 9/11, what was the prevalence of suicide?
Longitudinal study of the incidence of suicide attempts among women of Asian descent, with stillborn infants.

Correlational Study

Are reading comprehension scores associated with poverty levels in elementary school children?
Are types of pediatric cancer related to parental stress and coping strategies?
What variables predict perinatal depression?

Descriptive Study

To explore the socioeconomic and demographic characteristics of adolescents in behavioral correction high school programs.

To describe the interactions between visitors and nurses at the nursing station on post-surgical recovery wards in four local hospitals.

To better understand self-esteem among victims of abuse.

Case-Control Study

What factors contribute to the development of asthma in children under age five?

What are the differences between women who do and do not gain weight after hip-replacement surgery?

What differentiates females with Young Onset Parkinson's Disease from males with the condition?

Do males with bipolar disorder have a childhood trauma history that differs from a matched group of males without a psychiatric disorder?

Cohort Study – Prospective and Retrospective

Do adolescents' opinions about persons with mental illness change following exposure to education or information about psychiatric disorders?

Do children with food insecurities perform better academically after participating in a nutrition program?

Did symptoms of women with major depressive disorder improve following a program of cognitive behavioral therapy?

Case Study

Case studies increase our understanding of how a disease or condition presents, its etiology, and/or how it resolves under certain conditions.

If you have an interesting situation or set of conditions that beg for analysis and discussion with conclusions about lessons learned or further study recommendations, you may have the makings of a valuable Case Study.

For example: Munchausen Syndrome and Munchausen Syndrome by Proxy, Fibromyalgia, Physical illness that mimic mental disorders, or Recovery against the medical odds

Focused Literature Review

Are you interested in improving a clinical protocol or other practice? Or have you noticed common themes or unanswered questions in your area of interest?

A Focused Review of the literature may help uncover, reveal, or at least suggest a thematic pattern you can elucidate (clarify) in a new way. This may help readers to think differently about a topic or consider alternative methods of dealing effectively with a particular problem or condition.

Review studies of any clinical condition to sort out the variations in findings pertaining to any demographic, or to compile risk factors, rank them using a structured methodology, or organize them by demographics.

Review studies of a specific teaching method or framework to assess the frequency and scope of its use and examine whether outcome evaluations differ for the same method, and describe the outcomes across studies.

Survey Research

Opinions or information from a group that has not been studied, or that needs more study.

What are correctional officers' opinions of inmates with mental illness?

Do healthcare team members with interprofessional competencies have different attitudes toward unlike professions than those with no prior exposure to interprofessional training?

How do homeless men and women view their safety and s ecurity status?

How satisfied are first semester high school seniors with their prospects for education or employment after graduation?

References and Resources

This appendix contains references and resources. Keep in mind that although printed and e-books may be continuously available—permanently, perhaps—websites change, and what may be available today, may tomorrow be inaccessible, outdated, or no longer maintained.

Strengths and Limitations of non-experimental designs

Rezigalla, Assad A. 2020. "Observational Study Designs: Synopsis for Selecting an Appropriate Study Design." *Cureus*, January. https://doi.org/10.7759/cureus.6692.

Nadini Persaud, Dwayne Devonish, and Indeira Persaud. 2019. *Nuts & Bolts of Research Methodology: From Conceptualization to Write-Up*. Kingston, Jamaica: Ian Randle Publishers.

Motulsky, Harvey. 2018. *Intuitive Biostatistics: A Nonmathematical Guide to Statistical Thinking*. 4th ed. New York: Oxford University Press. http://www.intuitivebiostatistics.com/.

Schoonenboom, Judith, and R. Burke Johnson. 2017. "How to Construct a Mixed Methods Research Design." *KZfSS Kölner Zeitschrift Für Soziologie Und Sozialpsychologie* 69 (S2): 107–31. https://doi.org/10.1007/s11577-017-0454-1.

Liberati, A., D. G Altman, J. Tetzlaff, C. Mulrow, P. C Gotzsche, J. P A Ioannidis, M. Clarke, P J Devereaux, J. Kleijnen, and

D. Moher. 2009. "The PRISMA Statement for Reporting Systematic Reviews and Meta-Analyses of Studies That Evaluate Healthcare Interventions: Explanation and Elaboration." *BMJ* 339 (jul21 1): b2700–b2700. https://doi.org/10.1136/bmj.b2700.

Price, Paul C. 2017. "Research Methods in Psychology–Simple Book Publishing." Wsu.Edu. Pressbooks. August 21, 2017. https://opentext.wsu.edu/carriecuttler/.

"How to Apply - Application Guide | Grants.Nih.Gov." n.d. Grants.Nih.Gov. https://grants.nih.gov/grants/how-to-apply-application-guide.html#format.

The University of Minnesota has a website where you can gain more insight into the way to use or apply a study design. Access it at: https://libguides.umn.edu/c.php?g=999283

Lewallen, Susan, and P Courtright. "Epidemiology in Practice: Case-Control Studies." *Community Eye Health* 11, no. 28 (1998): 57–58.

Thalheimer, Will, and Samantha Cook. 2002. "How to Calculate Effect Sizes from Published Research: A Simplified Methodology." http://www.bwgriffin.com/gsu/courses/edur9131/content/Effect_Sizes_pdf5.pdf.

Olson, David H. 1986. "Circumplex Model VII: Validation Studies and FACES III." *Family Process* 25 (3): 337–51. https://doi.org/10.1111/j.1545-5300.1986.00337.x.

Olson, David H., Douglas H. Sprenkle, and Candyce S. Russell. 1979. "Circumplex Model of Marital and Family Systems: I. Cohesion and Adaptability Dimensions, Family Types, and Clinical Applications." *Family Process* 18 (1): 3–28. https://doi.org/10.1111/j.1545-5300.1979.00003.x.

Hildenbrand, Aimee K., Melissa A. Alderfer, Janet A. Deatrick, and Meghan L. Marsac. 2014. "A Mixed Methods Assessment of Coping with Pediatric Cancer." *Journal of Psychosocial Oncology* 32 (1): 37–58. https://doi.org/10.1080/07347332.2013.855960.

Frost, Jim. 2020. *Hypothesis Testing: An Intuitive Guide for Making Data Driven Decisions*. First. State College, PA: Statistics by Jim Publishing.

Frost, Jim. 2019. *Introduction to Statistics: An Intuitive Guide for Analyzing Data and Unlocking Discoveries*. State College, PA: Statistics by Jim Publishing.

Author's partial list of peer-reviewed publications

Zwickey, Heather, Heather Schiffke, Susan Fleishman, Mitch Haas, des Anges Cruser, Ron LeFebvre, Barbara Sullivan, Barry Taylor, and Barak Gaster. 2014. "Teaching Evidence-Based Medicine at Complementary and Alternative Medicine Institutions: Strategies, Competencies, and Evaluation." *The Journal of Alternative and Complementary Medicine* 20 (12): 925–31. https://doi.org/10.1089/acm.2014.0087.

Cruser, des Anges, Sarah K. Brown, Jessica R. Ingram, Frank Papa, Alan L. Podawiltz, David Lee, and Vesna Knox. 2012. "Practitioner Research Literacy Skills and abilities in Undergraduate Medical Education: Thinking Globally, Acting Locally." *Medical Science Educator* 22 (S3): 162–84. https://doi.org/10.1007/bf03341781.

Hall, Jessica M. F., desAnges Cruser, Alan Podawiltz, Diana I. Mummert, Harlan Jones, and Mark E. Mummert. 2012. "Psychological Stress and the Cutaneous Immune Response: Roles of the HPA Axis and the Sympathetic Nervous System in Atopic Dermatitis and Psoriasis." *Dermatology Research and Practice* 2012: 1–11. https://doi.org/10.1155/2012/403908.

Cruser, des Anges, Linda Asante-Ackuayi, Sarah Brown, Estela Cardenas, and David Lee. 2012. "Evidence-Based Guidance for Culturally Sensitive Assessment and Interventions for Perinatal Depression in Black American Women." *Journal of Primary Care & Community Health* 3 (4): 278–84. https://doi.org/10.1177/2150131912440454.

Cruser, des Anges, Douglas Maurer, Kendi Hensel, Sarah K Brown, Kathryn White, and Scott T Stoll. 2012. "A Randomized, Controlled Trial of Osteopathic Manipulative Treatment for Acute Low Back Pain in Active Duty Military Personnel." *Journal of Manual & Manipulative Therapy* 20 (1): 5–15. https://doi.org/10.1179/2042618611y.0000000016.

Cruser, des Anges, Sarah K Brown, Jessica R Ingram, Alan L Podawiltz, Bruce D Dubin, John S Colston, and Robert J Bulik. 2010. "Learning Outcomes from a Biomedical Research Course for Second Year Osteopathic Medical Students." *Osteopathic Medicine and Primary Care* 4 (1): 4. https://doi.org/10.1186/1750-4732-4-4.

Cruser, des Anges, Bruce Dubin, Sarah K Brown, Lori L Bakken, John C Licciardone, Alan L Podawiltz, and Robert J Bulik. 2009. "Biomedical Research Competencies for Osteopathic Medical Students." *Osteopathic Medicine and Primary Care* 3 (1): 10. https://doi.org/10.1186/1750-4732-3-10.

Cruser, des Anges, and Pamela M. Diamond. 2000. "Staff Opinions of Mentally Ill Offenders in a Prison Hospital: Implications for Training and Leadership." *Journal of Correctional Health Care* 7 (1): 127–47. https://doi.org/10.1177/107834580000700106.

Templates

Thank you for purchasing this book!

This appendix contains the image of the fillable forms that you may download free with your purchase of this book. Some of the formatting is lost in the imaging of the pdf templates. While you can write on these forms, the maximum benefit is from using the fillable templates.
Visit *ResearchProject-Help.com/templates* and enter password **mytools** to access your 13 fillable templates!

TEMPLATE 1: PROJECT FEASIBILITY CHECKLIST
Ideas, Advisors, Resources & Time Availability

This Template covers aspects of a research project you should consider in deciding if you can accomplish your goals. Use it to pre-plan and think through certain aspects of developing and conducting a research project, and prevent problems, or anticipate them and have a backup strategy.

Although there is no magic formula to determine if a project is feasible, and anything can happen, attending to them early can save you time, and improve the likelihood of success.

The best use of this form would be to type or write in your response to each item by yourself first, and then review them with your advisor. Together you may think of other questions that are important to answer before finalizing your project aim or research question, and beginning your project.

I. IDEAS AND ADVISORS

1. Do you have ideas for a project? Choose
   If you choose yes, enter them in this box below.

2. If you don't have clear ideas at this time, can you Choose
   identify at least one idea very soon?

3. What are some useful sources for your research project ideas? Check all that apply

   ☐ A professional lecture   ☐ Leisure reading

   ☐ Journal or reading club event   ☐ Professional interest article

   ☐ Journal article   ☐ News item

   ☐ Course lecture   ☐ Clinical experience

   ☐ Course reading   ☐ Grand Rounds presentation

   ☐ Other experience or content

1

4. What is the potential contribution of these ideas to your field? *Enter at least one contribution per idea on your list.*

5. What design most interests you? Select all that apply from the list.

☐	Case Control	☐	Exploratory & Developmental
☐	Cohort	☐	Case Study
☐	Cross-Sectional	☐	Survey Research as a developmental project
☐	Correlational		
☐	Focused review of the literature	☐	Qualitative
☐	Other:		

6. Do you have an advisor in your field of study? If you do, enter her/ his name here: Choose

7. Is a biostatistician willing to advise you? If ye, enter the person's name and contact information   Choose

8. Do you need other individuals as resources for your project?   Choose

   What roles will they fulfill?

2

II.   RESOURCES AND TIME

1. How long do you have or want to take to conduct this research?

2. Do I have authorized access to data or information?   Choose

Explain this situation below, or enter notes or action steps needed to secure access:

3. Do you have the necessary measurement instruments, questionnaires, or data collection forms?   Choose

    If Yes, what are they?

    If you don't have them, but know what they are, write them below, and what action you need to take to acquire them.

III.   GOALS, SCHEDULES, AND EXPECTATIONS

1. In the table on the next page, create a general list of goals you think you need to achieve or complete, finalize a plan, and finish the project. Then associate each goal and task with a timeline or deadline.

For example, find a biostatistician, finish my study question, meet with advisor to finalize plan, secure IRB approval.

If you prefer to include more details, use the table on the last page, Task and Schedule Master List with four column headings.

3

TEMPLATE 1
PROJECT FEASIBILITY CHECKLIST Ideas,
Advisors, Resources & Time Availability

GOALS AND TASKS	TIMELINE OR DEADLINE

4

PROJECT FEASIBILITY CHECKLIST Ideas,
Advisors, Resources & Time Availability

Flowchart Your Project

Step 1.   Right now, as you picture your project in your mind, draw <u>a flowchart of how you envision the research project steps, stages, or phases, and activities occurring</u>. This helps think about exactly what you will do to conduct and complete the project.
If you prefer not to draw, list all the steps, stages, phases, and activities you imagine will be needed to complete your research.

2. This task is a little harder: I want you to make list of the expectations you have of yourself and others that you believe are necessary to conduct and complete your project or study.

5

3. Describe the product/s you will create. *(For example, poster at research appreciation day, manuscript for publication, results section of a thesis, or presentation at specific venue/date)*

4. What, if any, adjustments do you need to make to feel comfortable that this project is feasible?

6

PROJECT FEASIBILITY CHECKLIST Ideas,
Advisors, Resources & Time Availability

Task and Schedule Master List			
What – Tasks	**Date**	**Who**	**Result or Product**
Pre-study example: Power analysis	*Meet on Monday January 15th*	*A biostatistician*	*Sample size*
Request electronic health record data	*Monday March 15th*	*Me and Info Systems contact*	*Clear expectations on data acquisition*
Example: Final interpretation of findings	*Tuesday May 20th*	*Me, Advisor, Statistician*	*Draft findings, data visualizations*

7

TEMPLATE 2. CORE SKILLS AND ABILITIES
Checklist, Planning, and Self-Rating

From the RPP Comprehensive Guide, you learned that you should have certain skills and abilities to tackle a research project. I've listed twenty core skills and abilities you should review prior to starting your project.

Rather than overlook the obvious, consider whether you are prepared to conduct research. Many of the skills I list in this template are those you should already have to perform the duties of your profession. But as humans, we all sometimes neglect to anticipate obstacles to our goals. When we confront those obstacles is the time we dig down deep and pull out latent skills or abilities we haven't had to use in a while.

If you can't organize materials, or sift through and discard nonessential information, or define your study variables, you may not be ready to develop a research project plan, and surely not ready to conduct research.

Review these twenty skills and abilities to consider whether you may need to acquire or strengthen any of them to confidently proceed to create a feasible, elegant project plan.

After the checklist, I've provided a rating scale for you to rate your level of confidence in each skill or ability. Following that self-rating scale, you'll find a guide to consider as you acquire or strengthen each of the twenty skills and abilities.

You can use this template to discuss the various skills and abilities with your advisor prior to beginning your planning document.

TEMPLATE 2. CORE SKILLS AND ABILITIES
Checklist, Planning, and Self-Rating

Core Skills and Abilities Checklist

#	I have this skill	I need this skill	Skills and Abilities
1	○	○	Knowledge of the topic of interest
2	○	○	Interest, curiosity about a specific observed phenomenon
3	○	○	Organization of thoughts (e.g., goal orientation, thinking skills, problem solving)
4	○	○	Analytic thinking**
5	○	○	Critical thinking**
6	○	○	Time Management (Scheduling, Planning)
7	○	○	Writing (Grammar, Structure, Logic)
8	○	○	General Vocabulary (comprehension)
9	○	○	Research Vocabulary (comprehension)
10	○	○	Patience (calm when obstacles arise, allowances for delays)
11	○	○	Diligence (careful, persistent, thorough)
12	○	○	Scanning a literature database efficiently
13	○	○	Excluding nonessential information to narrow the focus
14	○	○	Basic conversational knowledge of statistics
15	○	○	Human Subjects Protection principles and practices
16	○	○	Ethical (Honesty, Forthright, Judicious, Discrete, Fair)
17	○	○	Organization of tasks (space, transportation, resource acquisition)
18	○	○	Communication (Clarity of thought, verbal specificity)
19	○	○	Flexibility (Able to adjust to challenges, Creative – "outside the box" approaches to obstacles)
20	○	○	Integrity (Respectful, Truthful, Open minded)
AND		Identify any other skills and abilities you or your advisor believe are needed	

**Analytic thinking and critical thinking are sometimes confused. They are different mental activities with different purposes and outcomes.

TEMPLATE 2. CORE SKILLS AND ABILITIES
Checklist, Planning, and Self-Rating

Analytic thinking is the mental act of breaking down complex information, data, or facts into smaller parts for the purpose of organizing them and applying logic and reasoning to achieve a greater understanding of patterns, relationships, or other revelations. No judgment is involved. Activities involved in analytic thinking include:

1) Examining chunks of facts, data, or information and eliminating extraneous elements.
2) Applying logic to organize and sort information into meaningful sub-sets.
3) Identifying patterns or trends and considering relationships among the sub-sets.
4) Making observations.

Critical thinking involves mental activities engaging the right brain to evaluate information and interpret it using insight, perspective, context, and judgement. Analytic thinking is, however, an essential first step in the process of critical thinking. Activities involved in critical thinking include:

1) Collecting information, data, and facts about a clearly stated problem or issue.
2) Evaluating the credibility and accuracy of those data.
3) Applying analysis tools to understand the context, precipitating factors, or reasons for the stated problem.
4) Creatively analyzing information for a deeper understanding of a situation, or to generate researchable questions or theories, and formulate strategies to address the problem.

Acquiring or strengthening core skills and abilities

If you are concerned about your skill and ability to carry out a small scholarly project, consult with your advisor. S/he may have exactly the advice you need. You could also seek out a student-mentor-advisor who has completed a project of his or her own. S/he may share experiences with you that will help you decide how to acquire a particular skill that will enhance your success.

For example, if you don't have a general grasp of research language, reading published studies and discussing the articles with a group or an advisor will improve your skill and confidence. Or if you think you need to improve your writing skills for creating a research plan, critically reading other plans or grant proposals, or reports, will help you imitate an appropriate style.

Take a look at the self-rating scale on the following page. Set aside time for yourself to practice skills you may need to strengthen, such as being able to exclude nonessential information, or organizing your thoughts.

TEMPLATE 2. CORE SKILLS AND ABILITIES: CHECKLIST AND PLAN

Self-rating scale: Rate your competency in each skill and ability on a scale of 1 to 5, 5 being the most proficient. Use your self-rating scores to identify the skills and abilities needing the most attention. Give attention to your strengths. Try to be objective about your proficiencies and not too hard on yourself!

Skill or Ability	Rating
1) Knowledge of the topic of interest	5
2) Interest, curiosity about a specific observed phenomenon	5
3) Organization of thoughts (e.g., goal orientation, thinking skills, problem solving)	5
4) Analytic thinking**	5
5) Critical thinking**	5
6) Time Management (Scheduling, Planning)	5
7) Writing (Grammar, Structure, Logic)	5
8) General Vocabulary (comprehension)	5
9) Research Vocabulary (comprehension)	5
10) Patience (calm when obstacles arise, allowances for delays)	5
11) Diligence (careful, persistent, thorough)	5
12) Scanning a literature database efficiently	5
13) Excluding nonessential information to narrow the focus	5
14) Basic conversational knowledge of statistics	5
15) Human Subjects Protection principles and practices	5
16) Ethical (Honesty, Forthright, Judicious, Discrete, Fair)	5
17) Organization of tasks (space, transportation, resource acquisition)	5
18) Communication (Clarity of thought, verbal specificity)	5
19) Flexibility (Able to adjust to challenges, Creative – "outside the box" approaches to obstacles)	5
20) Integrity (Respectful, Truthful, Open minded)	5

TEMPLATE 3. FORMULATING THE STUDY QUESTION OR AIM

In this template there are two "mental process" cycles with four steps in each cycle, followed by two cycles of evaluating the availability of data and precision of the study question. Follow the steps below to create the best possible study question or aim.

Creating a measurable study question or aim is a journey. Be patient with yourself and the process. Keep your right brain engaged. Stop as needed to take a break, and pick it up later. Use the process and it will serve you well.

Mental Process Cycle One

Step 1. Observe. Make a statement about your topic of interest, using facts. Begin with *"Reports are...,"* or *"Research suggests that...,"* or a similar introductory phrase.

Step 2. Speculate. Make a statement about what you think about the observation, such as why you think it exists or occurs, or what it means. Begin with *"I think this is because...,"* or *"The reason this is happening or exists, may be..."*

Step 3. Question. Pose one or two initial research questions, based on your speculations. For a study aim, begin with *"The primary aim of this study is to..."* followed by a statement containing the same terms as a question, such as *"determine the extent to which X contributes to the presence of Y."* or *"to examine factors associated with Q."*

Step 4. Validate. Check the accuracy of the terms of your question or aim, by revisiting the literature or other source material. Is there truth in your speculation and subsequent question? Is it on target? Is there information that suggests we already have the answer?

1

TEMPLATE 3. FORMULATING THE STUDY QUESTION OR AIM

Step 5. **Observe.** Revisit your observation with increased focus, using the information you found from returning to source materials.

```
 
 
 
```

Step 6. **Speculate.** With increased focus, write what you think about the nature of your refocused observation, incorporating new information into what you think about it.

```
 
 
 
```

Step 7. **Question.** Reformulate your initial question/s or study aim to narrow the topic, and be more specific about key facets of your speculation.

```
 
 
 
```

Step 8. **Validate.** Using your revised question, reexamine the literature and source materials to drill down to a smaller arena, or to exclude extraneous variables. What do you discover? How does new information affect your revised question or speculations?

```
 
 
 
```

NOTE: If you keep your current question or aim, proceed to step 9. If you decide to revise it, type it here.

```
 
 
 
```

2

TEMPLATE 3. FORMULATING THE STUDY QUESTION OR AIM

Step 9. Consider data availability: If you cannot obtain data for the project as it is currently defined, you'll want to revise the question. Even if you can obtain those data, you should then carefully consider the size and scope of the project that the current question sets up.

a. Complete the table. Determine if you have access to the data your study would require.

Variables	Definition	Source

b. **Question reformulation.** On the basis of whether you can collect data for the variables you just listed, consider those in which you have the most interest, to revise the study question, with even greater specificity. Enter it below, and use it for Step 10. If you keep your question, enter it here and proceed to Step 12.

Step 10.   Reconsider data availability. If you modified your question based on data availability, revise the list of variables based on that new question. NOTE: If you have more than eight variables, you may have too many. Thing about each variable. For example, if self-esteem has ten items in a questionnaire, there are ten items for each case to enter. If you have two surveys or measurement instruments your data entry increases. It is possible that your analysis potential is also greater, so consider what and whether you need all variables in the interest of keeping the project size modest relative to collecting and managing the data.

3

TEMPLATE 3. FORMULATING THE STUDY QUESTION OR AIM

Variables	Definition	Source

Step 11. Finalize your study question or aim. Make certain that the question can be measured, the project is not so large as to be unfeasible, and that the scope is narrow enough to be meaningful.

This may seem like a redundant step, but consider that every time you read your study question aloud, it has a rhythm, a message. Is it specific enough for the project to be feasible – not too broad in scope, and not too large in terms of data collection or task demands?

Review this with your advisor, and you're good to go!

TEMPLATE 4. THE LITERATURE SEARCH:
SEVEN POINTS FOR PREPAREDNESS

If you have never done a literature search, this template will help you prepare for the process. Even if you have experience with literature searches, this will refresh your skills. Answer each question with as much information as possible.

1. Are there any existing published "reviews of the literature" on my topic?

Yes ◯   No ◯

Action: If there are, list them here by last name & initials of the first author, date, and title.

```
```

If you have a printed binder, print the article. Otherwise, download the pdf to add to your e-binder.

2. Are there textbooks or chapters in published textbooks on this subject, in addition to published peer review articles, that I might use?

Yes ◯   No ◯

Action: If these exist, get access to them for your reference list or acquire them for your bookshelf.

3. Do non-academic or unpublished materials exist on this topic that I should consider? These would be for example, policies, minutes of meetings, management databases, or conference papers.

Yes ◯   No ◯

Actions: If these exist, get access to them for your reference list or bookshelf.

4. Is there an underlying theoretical or contextual framework that defines my topic of interest?

Yes ◯   No ◯

Actions: Summarize the framework here, with appropriate references

```
```

Action: Acquire the articles that document the framework.

1

TEMPLATE 4. THE LITERATURE SEARCH:
SEVEN POINTS FOR PREPAREDNESS

5. Who is the librarian who will help me create my key word list, and conduct an efficient, targeted search of databases, and what is the contact information?

6. What databases and key words do I think I will use for my first dive into the literature?

7. What electronic file system or printed notebook format will I use to create an organized compendium of materials?

8. Are there other considerations I must address to be able to conduct an efficient, focused, thorough, and credible literature search for my study?

2

TEMPLATE 5. SOURCE MATERIALS - FIVE CONSIDERATIONS
Determining the value of source material for your research project

This template provides five considerations to help you determine if a research report is relevant and applicable to your project. Your responses to these considerations will guide your selection of research reports that are most closely related to your study. Respond to every question within each consideration, and follow the instructions.

Before you begin check off these steps.

☐ **Step 1.** Identify and acquire the pdfs or printed copies of no more than three of the most recently published studies specifically and directly associated with your topic or question.

☐ **Step 2:** Read them. Be sure you understand the analysis and findings for each study. Seek guidance if you need clarification.

☐ **Step 3:** Refer to these articles as you respond to each consideration.

Consideration #1

To be useful for your project, any journal article or research report must support four tasks.

Task a) Refining your study question.

Task b) Supporting the importance of your project.

Task c) Selecting a suitable design or structure for your project.

Task d) Assessing the need for a power analysis, number of cases or subjects, and data analysis methods.

Question: Is all the information listed below contained in these published studies?

☐ Topic	☐ Design
☐ Study question or aim	☐ Methods
☐ Population	☐ Analysis
☐ Sample size	☐ Limitations
☐ Primary outcome	☐ Findings
☐ Measurement instruments detailed	☐ Significance
☐ Variables	☐ Effect size
☐ Intervention or hypothesized explanatory variable (optional)	

Proceed to the next page.

TEMPLATE 5. SOURCE MATERIALS - FIVE CONSIDERATIONS
Determining the value of source material for your research project

Step 1: If you have not found all the necessary information in the articles you have, choose a or b.

(a) Refine your search terms or your question. Select different source materials. Review Consideration #1 again.

(b) Make an attempt to address Consideration #2.
    Example: You've found a study of factors contributing to recovery in post knee arthroscopy athletes, but your interest is in knee replacement in a variety of age groups. What should you do? You can keep the article, examine the citations to determine if there is a study more similar to your ideas, find them and review them, then discard the original article. Or you can restructure your search terms to exclude athletes or arthroscopic surgery.

Instructions
After you have met both of these criteria*
* You have at least two articles with all the information in Consideration #1.
* You verify that the information relates specifically and directly to your project.
Then proceed to address Consideration #2.

Consideration #2

Check each item that applies to the sources you are using.

☐ These studies have the same population as my study.

☐ These studies use the same variables as I want to use.

☐ These studies provide adequate evidence that my study has value.

☐ I can use the statistics in these articles to work with a biostatistician for my study's design and methodology. (*Note: You only need two articles that meet this criterion.*)

☐ I can use these articles or materials as a comparison for my results. (*Note: You only need one article that meets this criterion.*)

Instructions
*If you **have not checked** all the items above, take the following actions.*
Revise your study question and/or
Revise your search terms.
Then begin at the first consideration with your new materials.
*If you **have checked** all the items in Consideration #2, proceed to Consideration #3.*

TEMPLATE 5. SOURCE MATERIALS - FIVE CONSIDERATIONS
Determining the value of source material for your research project

Consideration #3

Does this criterion apply to the articles you have?

☐ I can use at least some of the sources cited by the authors in these studies, for writing the background section and providing support for my study.

Instructions

If none of the citations in the studies you have selected are related specifically and directly to your project, they will not contribute valuable information to your Background & Importance section. Review the articles you have with your advisor to ensure they meet your needs.

If you have checked the box for Consideration #3, take the actions below.

Action Step 1: Using the authors' citations, acquire not more than six of the articles most germane to your question, including any seminal works (foundational, groundbreaking).

Action Step 2: Read the abstracts.

Action Step 3: Address items a. through d. below.

a) How do the conclusions in each article underscore or point to the direction I am taking with my project?

b) What trends in the research, and/or recommendations for future directions support the rationale for my project?

TEMPLATE 5. SOURCE MATERIALS - FIVE CONSIDERATIONS
Determining the value of source material for your research project

c) What gaps in the knowledge do the authors identify, and how do those gaps link to their recommendations for further research?

d) Check again to determine if there are any <u>more recent</u> papers with additional research on the topic. If you find any, look at the abstract to determine their relevance to your study. If they are useful, enter the citations here.

Instructions
Proceed to Consideration #4

Consideration #4

Does this condition apply to you?

☐ I have sufficient material for my Background & Importance section.

Instructions

If you didn't check the box, you may need more information to fully explain the background and importance of your project. You'll conduct a complete search of the literature.

If you checked the box, you can consider ending your literature search.

Before you decide to end your search, consider the following three points.

Point 1: If your advisor requires an exhaustive search, or if your advisor has published in this topic, you may need to search further.

TEMPLATE 5. SOURCE MATERIALS - FIVE CONSIDERATIONS
Determining the value of source material for your research project

Point 2: There may be value in acquiring information from fact-based, reliable, and valid web-based sources such as national, state, or local statistics or reporting agencies.

Point 3: When you begin to see citations repeated in articles you review, you likely have exhausted the available publications in this topic.

Consideration #5

Conflicting viewpoints on the topic. If you have not found any, explore other materials that might refute, or dispute the findings you have. If they exist, you will need them for your Background & Importance section. *Don't overlook different aspects of the same topic, such as studies of the condition of interest in a different population than you are considering.*

Make any additional notes you need in the text box below, to keep track of your decisions in these five considerations.

TEMPLATE 6. CRITICAL ANALYSIS OF A RESEARCH ARTICLE

This template has 27 items that will guide you through identifying and recording the key elements of a research study. The information you will record in this template helps you identify similarities between the published study you are analyzing, and your project. When you evaluate the information, you will be able to generate a substantial list of possible study variables to include or exclude in your project. Comparing your list to those in the study or studies on which your project rests may generate additional variables, or possibly eliminate some.

Complete the information called for in each item.

1. The last name, first name, or initials of the first author.

2. The title and date of article or materials.

3. The topic.

4. The study's Primary Question, Aim, Goal, and/or Hypothesis.

5. What is the importance of this study?

6. What is the theoretical framework for the study?

7. What is the target population with inclusion and exclusion criteria, if relevant?

8. What is the primary outcome variable, and what are the other variables in the study?

TEMPLATE 6. CRITICAL ANALYSIS OF A RESEARCH ARTICLE

9. Name the study design, structure, or approach.

10. Do you think the design is the best one to address the research question or achieve the study aim or goal?

Yes ☐   No ☐

Why did you select yes or no?

If you selected no, and you think it could or should be conducted using a different approach, what approach would you use?

11. Briefly summarize how the author evaluated the literature so as to provide an acceptable rationale for the study.

12. If there is opposing, conflicting, or controversial information about the topic or research question or goals, did the author include it, and how is it addressed?

13. If you wanted to know more about the study, could you find it based on information in the article?

Yes ☐   No ☐

Where would you find it?

14. How did the researcher measure the primary outcome or condition of interest?

TEMPLATE 6. CRITICAL ANALYSIS OF A RESEARCH ARTICLE

15. What information does the article provide about validity and reliability information for the measurement tools or methods?

16. If the research used new, novel, or innovative measurement tools, what are they, and how to they help answer the question?

17. If the research was to develop a new intervention or measurement tool, how did the authors go about the process?

18. What conclusions are most useful, and does the author speculate about or interpret study findings?

19. List the steps you believe the researchers would have taken to conduct and complete the study.

20. Considering the conclusions, narratively deconstruct or trace the flow of the discussion, noting if you find any gaps in or leaps of logic.

21. In what ways does this study contribute to our understanding of the topic, problem, or phenomenon?

22. What are the strengths and limitations of the study?

TEMPLATE 6. CRITICAL ANALYSIS OF A RESEARCH ARTICLE

23. How does this material support your study aim?

24. What specific information will you use from this source to shape, construct, organize, conduct, and complete your study?

25. What did you like <u>best</u> about this study?

26. What did you like the <u>least</u> about this study?

27. Additional notes for your use:

TEMPLATE 7. IN-DEPTH ANALYSIS OF SOURCE MATERIAL

YOUR NAME: _____   DATE: _____

PRIMARY AUTHOR (LAST, INITIALS) _____

SOURCE TITLE_____

> **Step One: Read the abstract, then answer the next eight questions.**

1) What is your study topic or population of interest?
   _____

2) What topic or population does this research study?
   _____

3) Is this a U.S. Study? If not, what country?
   Yes ◯   No ◯   Other _____

4) What is the rationale for this study? Why is it important?
   _____

5) Is this a global, or local (what country, and community) concern?
   ☐ Global   ☐ Local _____

6) What study design do the researchers use?
   ☐ Case-Control   ☐ Experimental
   ☐ Cross-sectional   ☐ Cohort
   ☐ Correlational   ☐ Focused Review of the Literature
   ☐ Meta-Analysis   ☐ Other _____

7) What is the primary research question and/or study hypothesis?
   _____

8) What is your decision, based on your review of the abstract?
   This article is useful for my study   ◯ Yes   ◯ No
   This article is useful for other reasons.   ◯ Yes   ◯ No
   Keep it?   ◯ Yes   ◯ No

TEMPLATE 7. IN-DEPTH ANALYSIS OF SOURCE MATERIAL

> **Step Two: Scan or read the article, then answer each question below.**

PURPOSE, TYPE OF STUDY, QUESTION, HYPOTHESIS

9) What is the primary outcome of interest or focus/objective of the study?

_____

10) What describes the purpose of this study? (Select all that apply)

☐ Increase our understanding of health status issues in areas such as risk, incidence, or prevalence

☐ Increase our scientific understanding of a health related condition, disease etiology, or a treatment method

☐ Report on the results of a randomized clinical trial

☐ Examine or explain behaviors, opinions, procedures, or other phenomena

☐ Other

11) Based on the background information, this study is intended to:

☐ Provide new treatment choices or methods.

☐ Increase our understanding of the topic.

☐ Refute previous reports or findings.

☐ Confirm previous reports or findings.

☐ Provide information for guiding health care policy and practice.

☐ Build new or improved theories on the topic.

☐ Other

12) What type of study is this?

☐ Descriptive   ☐ Existing data or using data in a novel way

☐ Survey or interviews   ☐ Experimental

☐ Policy or services research   ☐ Exploratory or pilot research

☐ Clinical trial   ☐ Systematic review or meta-analysis

☐ Other

TEMPLATE 7. IN-DEPTH ANALYSIS OF SOURCE MATERIAL

OUTCOMES AND STUDY DESIGN

13) Are there other questions or hypotheses in addition to the primary one? (Refer to #7 on page 1)

      Yes ◯   No ◯

      If yes, what are they? _____

14) How did the researchers measure the primary outcome or the primary construct/object of interest?

☐ Directly assessed with subjective tool or questionnaire

☐ Directly assessed with objective methods

☐ Indirectly assessed using available data

☐ Another method. _____

15) What types of data are collected to measure the primary outcome or study objective?

Nominal ☐   Ordinal ☐   Continuous (Interval or Ratio Scale) ☐

16) What secondary outcomes or measurements were studied? What types of variables were used to measure each secondary outcome?

Identified Secondary Outcomes	Nominal	Ordinal	Continuous (Interval or Ratio Scale)
1.	◯	◯	◯
2.	◯	◯	◯
3.	◯	◯	◯

17) Look at the study design you selected in #6 on page 1, or look in the article for the study design. Why do you believe the authors selected that design?

    To measure the effects of one or more experimental methods

    To investigate how or why one group developed a condition compared to another group that did not develop the condition

    To determine what factors appear to best explain an observed phenomenon or condition

    To determine changes in specific conditions over time

    To explore the topic or condition to better understand it.

    Hypothesis generating   Inductive process or theory building

    Other _____

TEMPLATE 7. IN-DEPTH ANALYSIS OF SOURCE MATERIAL

POPULATIONS AND INTERVENTIONS

18) What population(s) did the researchers include?

Elderly specify age range _____	Adults not-elderly, over 25 ☐
Young adults (18-25) ☐	Adolescents (12-18) ☐
Children under age 12 ☐	Healthy (normal) population ☐
Specific race, ethnic group, or nationality _____	Population with a specific clinical ☐ condition
Specific socioeconomic group	Other _____

19) How did the researchers obtain or draw their sample? (Select one best response)

☐ No sampling method was used   ☐ Convenience sample

☐ Existing data   ☐ Random sample from defined population

☐ Other notes about the study sample/population: _____

20) Population and sample:

Eligible Population	Number in the study	Number excluded, dropped, or lost	Final sample size

21) Did the study include control or experimental groups?   YES   NO

If YES, which ones?

Treatment or Intervention Group ☐   Condition Present ☐

Comparison groups ☐   Condition not Present ☐

Other: notes about study groups

22) Did this study include an intervention or a treatment?   YES ◯   NO ◯

If yes, what was it?

TEMPLATE 7. IN-DEPTH ANALYSIS OF SOURCE MATERIAL

DATA AND ANALYSIS

23) What were the sources of data for this study?

☐ Clinical Observation or Opinion ☐ Clinical Rating Tool or Scale

☐ Existing Data from a data set ☐ Health Records

☐ Interviews ☐ Mailed Survey or Questionnaire

☐ Medical or Lab Tests ☐ Other

24) Were there any special methods or precautions used to ensure study integrity? (e.g. sampling methods, inclusion or exclusion criteria, matching subjects)

☐ Blinding researchers ☐ Blinding study participants

☐ Matching criteria applied ☐ Subjects were randomized to groups

☐ Standardized and validated measurement tools ☐ Treatment or intervention was randomized

☐ Other _____

25) What statistical tests did researchers use to address the PRIMARY study question (test the hypothesis)?

☐ ANOVA (Analysis of Variance)

☐ Chi-square

☐ Confidence Intervals

☐ Correlation (Pearson, Spearman, Kendall, etc)

☐ Descriptive statistics only

☐ Factor analysis (variable reduction and structure detection methods)

☐ Regression

☐ Non-parametric tests (e.g. Wilcoxon, Mann-Whiney, Kruskal Wallis)

☐ Survival Analysis

☐ T-test

☐ Test of agreement or concordance (e.g. Cohen's Kappa, intra-class correlation)

☐ Other: _____

TEMPLATE 7. IN-DEPTH ANALYSIS OF SOURCE MATERIAL

DATA AND ANALYSIS CONTINUED

26) Why did the researchers select those statistics?

☐ To measure change over time   ☐ Create prediction models

☐ To measure differences between groups   ☐ Estimate prevalence or incidence

☐ Explore relationships among variables   ☐ Measure time to an event

☐ Other: _____

27) What is the main result or finding?

_____

28) Was the primary hypothesis supported or rejected, and can you explain why?

○ Supported   ○ Rejected

Why? _____

29) Did any secondary outcome findings support, refute, or elucidate the primary findings?

○ Yes   ○ No

If "yes," how? _____

30) What strengths of the study make this suitable for your purposes?

_____

31) What limitations of the study raise cautions about using this study for your purposes?

_____

32) What contribution does this research make to your field of interest?

_____

33) Based on this article, write one or two questions you think would constitute suitable future directions for this area of research.

_____

TEMPLATE 8.
CONSTRUCTING THE BACKGROUND & IMPORTANCE SECTION

In this template you will work through each of the ten points that need to be covered in the B&I section of the plan. Keep in mind the following guiding principles for constructing this section of the plan, as you work through each point.

Guiding Principles for Writing the Background & Importance Section

---

Be specific: guide the reader from the statement of your question or hypothesis into a discussion of its history and importance.

Populate each point with references to published studies or other source materials.

Use connective and conclusion phrases to move through the narrative.

Use contrasts, comparisons, and links between and among the studies you have chosen as most supportive and contradictory, if relevant, to your project.

Construct your responses using complete sentences. For each statement you make, refer to and cite the article where you found the information.

---

1. **The topic and the most important facts about the topic:** Write one or two sentences.

2. **The study question or aim:** Write a "therefore" sentence containing your study aim or question.

3. **The scientific basis or principles,** clinical or theoretical framework for your study: summarize it in one or two sentences referring to it as the basis for your study.

4. **Summarize seminal or foundational studies:** Write one or two sentences about the origins of the theoretical framework, or how it initiated the movement, framework, or theory.

5. **Latest published research on the topic.** You should cover only the three to five most recently published studies, although you may say there are X number of articles or sources, but too many to cover in this section.

6. **Gaps in the knowledge:** Write two sentences as appropriate.

7. **Filling the gaps:** Write one to two sentences describing how your study will fill the gaps.

8. **Benefits to studying the topic:** Write one to two sentences describing the benefits of acquiring additional knowledge or understanding of the topic as you are approaching it.

9. **Conflicting information:** Write one or two sentences as it relates to your project.

10. **How does the literature support the rationale for your study?** Make this one or two sentences that will link into the Structure & Methods section. Start with "therefore," or "in summary."

Template 9. Biostatistician Meeting Checklist and Agenda

Use this template to prepare the information and agenda for your meetings with a biostatistician or statistics advisor. You will enter data to prepare for the meeting, and record the results of your discussions. The information in this template will help you when you construct the Structure & Methods section of the Research Project Plan, and prepare for your human subjects' research protocol application.

Step 1. Variables list

In the table below, enter the variables you have finalized from item Templates 3 or 6, or list the variables you think you will use, still in preliminary form. Try to keep the number of variables under ten.

Table: Study Variables

Variable	Definition	Source

Step 2. Sampling, or Population Inclusion and Exclusion Criteria

INCLUSION	EXCLUSION
Example: Enrolled or registered in the sixth grade	*Example: All other grade school classes*
Example: Post-partum females between the ages of 21 and 35 at the time of delivery	*Example: All women below the age of 21, and over the age of 35*

Step 3. One or two published studies most like your own. Enter the citation/s.

Template 9. Biostatistician Meeting Checklist and Agenda

Step 4. Identify the key elements in each benchmark study.

<u>Journal Article One</u>

<u>First author's last name:</u>

Statistic or Element	Quantity or Definition
Study Population; Number of cases	
Primary study question	
Primary Outcome Variable	
Number of study cases or participants	
Statistical test	
Effect size	
P-value	

<u>Journal Article Two</u>

<u>First author's last name:</u>

Statistic or Element	Quantity or Definition
Study Population; Number of cases	
Primary study question	
Primary Outcome Variable	
Number of study cases or participants	
Statistical test	
Effect size	
P-value	

Additional notes:

Template 9. Biostatistician Meeting Checklist and Agenda

Step 5. Agenda for meeting with a biostatistician. (Enter your information into the text boxes, and check these when completed.) Take the articles with you to your meetings.

☐ Refine and finalize the definition of each variable. (Specific Aims, Background and Importance, and Methods)

☐ Ensure that each variable is appropriately defined, and if it is a surrogate, verify that it is a valid and reliable surrogate. (Methods)

☐ Document the results of the power analysis. (Power Analysis)

☐ Determine how many cases you need to have confidence in the statistical tests for addressing your study question or aim. (Power Analysis)

☐ Determine what statistical tests are best suited to address your question or aim, considering the types of data you will have. (Methods)

☐ Identify the statistical software that will be used for the analysis. (Methods).

☐ Discuss your study's integrity in the form of strengths and limitations.

Step 6. Revise the table on page 2 of this template to create your final list of variables.

3

TEMPLATE 10. STRUCTURE & METHODS

By completing this template you will have addressed all the narrative elements you need for the Structure & Methods section of your Research Project Plan. There are nine major parts to this section, including Human Subjects Protection elements.

A. INTRODUCTION AND ORGANIZATION OF MATERIAL

    1. Restate the research aims, question, or hypothesis, including a statement about the topic and the population.

    2. Describe the approach you are taking to achieve the study aim or address the question.

    3. What information are you providing in this narrative? How is this section organized?

B. STUDY DESIGN OR PROJECT STRUCTURE

    1. What is the research design or structure?

    2. Why have you selected this approach? *Be specific, ensure the study structure suits the question.*

C. POWER ANALYSIS: From your meeting with a biostatistician, enter the following information.

    1. What effect size are you targeting?

    2. How many cases or subjects do you need?

    3. If the study is not responsive to the power analysis, explain why, and how it affects the study.

1

TEMPLATE 10. STRUCTURE & METHODS

D. CASES OR STUDY SUBJECTS/PARTICIPANTS

1. Criteria for inclusion and exclusion

INCLUSION	EXCLUSION
Example: Enrolled or registered in the sixth grade	*Example: All other grade school classes*
Example: Post-partum females between the ages of 21 and 35 at the time of delivery	*Example: All women below the age of 21, and over the age of 35*

2. How will you draw the sample or recruit study participants?

E. OUTCOME MEASURES AND DATA COLLECTION

1. Complete the table below with your final list of study data you will collect.

Variables	Definition	Source

2

TEMPLATE 10. STRUCTURE & METHODS

2. Using your checklist for data collection planning, write a statement summarizing the methods you will use. (Limit yourself to two or three sentences)

F. DATA MANAGEMENT AND ANALYSIS

1. What software will you use for data management?

2. Describe any plans and any necessary stages for sequencing and completing data entry.

3. How will you store and secure and protect data?

4. How will you approach the analysis and interpretation of findings? Include any collaboration or guidance.

G. PROJECT MANAGEMENT PLAN AND TIMELINES

1. What time do you have to conduct the study? *Be specific, such as two hours week for three months, or two days a week for six months. Calculate the total number of hours you have available. Account for any potential obstacles.*

3

TEMPLATE 10. STRUCTURE & METHODS

2. Complete the table below. List all the steps to conduct and complete the project.

TASKS	TIME REQUIREMENTS

3. List and annotate any other resources you need, such as permissions, passcodes, flash drives, CDs, transportation, meeting space?

4. What happens after you have the results? How will you report them?

H. **STUDY INTEGRITY: What makes it a valid or trustworthy project? What are its strengths and limitations, such as number of subjects or cases, missing data, can't be generalized to other schools, or other age groups. <u>Every study</u> has limitations and strengths.**

4

TEMPLATE 10. STRUCTURE & METHODS

I. HUMAN SUBJECTS' PROTECTION: Is the review complete? Do you have all required approvals? If you do not have your approvals, what do you need to do to apply or complete the process? What procedures must you follow for protection of subjects or their information?

J. Be sure to create your project management plan and timeline table, and make notes in this text box about any other requirements there may be for your project.

5

TEMPLATE 11. DATA COLLECTION AND MANAGEMENT PLANNING

You have your list of variables and specifically how you have defined them. Now you want to collect those numbers or other information that will become the data set for your study.

Before you begin, you need to have the answers to ten minimally crucial questions. Completing each item below will cover all ten. Note, that for your project, you may need to go beyond these questions, including for example, considering whether you will need transportation to go to a site to collect data, or provide drop-boxes for surveys.

Let's begin your data collection and data management strategies.

1. What data will you collect on each study variable, and from what source? Try to limit the number of study variables to 10 or fewer.

Variable	Definition	Source

2. Do I have authorized access? YES ◯   NO ◯

3. If you do not have access at this time, do you know how to acquire access?

YES ◯   NO ◯

Describe your strategy to acquire access or permissions.

TEMPLATE 11. DATA COLLECTION AND MANAGEMENT PLANNING

4. In the table below identify the data sources and other information for each column heading.

Data Source	Request Needed?	Format/Structure	Anticipated Receipt Date

5. For each variable whose data I will collect myself, directly from a paper or electronic source, where, how, and using what tools will I do that?

6. If you have questionnaires or survey forms, or tests, enter the details in the table below.

Measurement Instrument	Format	Have or Need

TEMPLATE 11. DATA COLLECTION AND MANAGEMENT PLANNING

7. For each measurement instrument, enter information about distribution, collection, and storage.

Measurement Instrument	Distribution and Collection	Storage

8. What else should I be aware of, or attend to, that affects the collection and management of the study data?

TEMPLATE 12. SPECIFIC AIMS

To write this section, you need to have these five items. They can be draft, but you'll need all of them to write this section.

1. An impactful statement about the importance of the topic your study addresses.
2. Your primary research question <u>and</u> its corollary null hypothesis
3. A high-level statement of why you want to study this question and the broader implications for the field
4. A summary of your methods
5. Your punch line

1) Write an introduction. Example: *A normal human brain does not fully develop until young adulthood. Certain cognitive functions that may appear impaired in adolescents are actually simply not present. Questions persist about what determines if a youth goes to juvenile detention or to a psychiatric unit for treatment regardless of the precipitating behaviors.*

2) Write your primary research aim and/or question as a sentence. Example: *I propose to increase our understanding of the role cognitive functioning may have in the incarceration-treatment outcome for adolescent girls and boys in the local county institutions.*

And, write the null hypothesis. Example: *My hypothesis is that there is no significant difference in cognitive functioning between the two groups. As a secondary question, I will evaluate the relationship between placement outcome and precipitating behavior.*

3) Write a high-level statement of why you want to study this question. Example: *Correctional systems and mental health systems tend not to share information about the adolescents in their care and custody. This prevents effective care coordination and may be an obstacle to achieving desirable health outcomes. If cognitive functioning does not differ between incarcerated and hospitalized youth, but precipitating behavior explains the placement, interventions for both groups could effectively include cognitive behavioral therapy.*

TEMPLATE 12. SPECIFIC AIMS

4) Write summary sentences describing your methods. Example: *Both systems collect and retain cognitive functioning test scores for the adolescent populations they serve. With appropriate approvals I will use de-identified data for this study. Approximately fifty cases are available in each system. This number of subjects provides sufficient cases for There may be duplicate cases, in which situation, a secondary analysis of test score differences will be performed. Because of the small sample size, there is a higher chance for a Type II error that is missing a difference or effect when there truly is one. I will use t-tests for the main hypothesis, and analysis of variance tests for sub-group analyses. Graphical displays such as scatterplots will add depth to the analysis process.*

5) Write your punch line. Example: *Better understanding the cognitive differences or similarities between incarcerated and hospitalized adolescents could change the way therapists apply cognitive therapy principles in each milieu.*

Make any other notes you want to consider or include in the Specific Aims section of your project plan.

TEMPLATE 13. PLAN NARRATIVE:
ASSEMBLING THE DOCUMENT

Purpose and use

This template provides an outline that will pull together all the sections of your project plan. There are six components.

    A. Study Question/Aim, and Design/Structure
    B. Literature, Background & Importance
    C. Variables and Data Management
    D. Structure & Methods
    E. Human Subjects, Protection and Ethics
    F. Scheduling Tasks

Follow the steps to your best advantage. When you are finished, you can copy and paste the narratives you've created into a word document or other text file for a seamless final draft for editing .

A. STUDY QUESTION/AIM AND DESIGN/STRUCTURE

First, work through these preliminary context considerations to get in the groove.

1. Type in your professional field of interest and the subject of your research project. For example, psychology, and trauma.

2. State the target phenomenon and population for your study. For example, psychological trauma in post-discharged trauma-center patients.

   - What are the characteristics of the population? For example, all races and ethnic groups, or single mothers.

   - What are the specific aspects of the conditions in that population that spark your curiosity? For example, while a single mother is hospitalized, what happens to her family, and what are her worries or problems?

   - Describe the physical, psychological or social construct that interests you, such as diabetes, self-esteem, executive functioning, family systems, or poverty.

TEMPLATE 13. PLAN NARRATIVE:
ASSEMBLING THE DOCUMENT

Task and Schedule Master List			
What – Tasks	**Date**	**Who**	**Result or Product**
Pre-study example: Power analysis	Meet on Monday, January 15th	A biostatistician	Sample size
Request electronic health record data	Monday, March 15th	Me and Info Systems contact	Clear expectations on data acquisition
Example: Final interpretation of findings	Tuesday, May 20th	Me, Advisor, Statistician	Draft findings, data visualizations

TEMPLATE 13. PLAN NARRATIVE: ASSEMBLING THE DOCUMENT

- Describe the relationship/s that most interest you in the population associated with the condition/s. (Think about how variables, characteristics, behaviors, opinions, or conditions interact.)

3. Now enter your study question or aim, using *Template 3. Formulating the Study Question or Aim.*

4. Using the information from *Template 12*, write your entire Specific Aims section here.

TEMPLATE 13. PLAN NARRATIVE: ASSEMBLING THE DOCUMENT

B. LITERATURE, BACKGROUND & IMPORTANCE

Referring to the information in *Template 8 Constructing the Background & Importance*, write a complete narrative that smoothly connects and covers the ten points.

TEMPLATE 13. PLAN NARRATIVE: ASSEMBLING THE DOCUMENT

C. VARIABLES AND STUDY POPULATION

Step 1. Complete the table below as a final, based on your meetings with a biostatistician and your advisor. You have entered this information in several templates, so by now, you should have the shortest list possible.

Study Variables

Variable	Definition	Source

Step 2. Write a statement about the population for the study, the inclusion and exclusion criteria, and how you are enrolling study participants or sampling cases.

TEMPLATE 13. PLAN NARRATIVE:
ASSEMBLING THE DOCUMENT

D. STRUCTURE AND METHODS

For this section, use the information from Templates 10 and 11.

Step 1. Introduction: restate the purpose of the study and why you choose the approach you will describe in this section of the plan. (Template 10, A, 1-3)

Step 2.   Pull your statements from Template 10, item B 1–2 into a narrative structure for design and rationale.

Step 3.   Create a sentence, or two at the most, using your answers to items C 1–3, in Template 10, and any information you entered in *Template 9, Biostatistician Meeting Checklist and Agenda,* to summarize the power analysis, number of subjects/cases, and whether your study will meet the target.

Step 4.   Create one or two sentences about the variables. Use the information in section C of this template, and information from Template 9, 10, or 11. They should all be consistent, but double check your notes. Also, to be clear, you only need to discuss the key study variables in this plan section, as you will have a complete list in the IRB protocol, and you may collect more data than you will analyze for this particular study question.

TEMPLATE 13. PLAN NARRATIVE:
ASSEMBLING THE DOCUMENT

Step 5. Use information in items E 2–5 in Template 10, to create a narrative of how you will collect, enter, and store study data.

Step 6. Use the table below to enter list all the forms you will use to collect data, even if it is in the form of a request for electronic files.

DCF	Method
Spreadsheet for abstracting demographics, diagnosis, and test scores from the electronic health record.	*I will hand copy the data from X office computer.*

Step 7. Construct one or two sentences using the information from Template 10, item E 6 about your approach to analysis of data.

TEMPLATE 13. PLAN NARRATIVE:
ASSEMBLING THE DOCUMENT

Step 8. Combine all the narrative from steps 1 – 7 above into one complete Structure & Methods section.

TEMPLATE 13. PLAN NARRATIVE:
ASSEMBLING THE DOCUMENT

Task and Schedule Master List			
What – Tasks	**Date**	**Who**	**Result or Product**
Pre-study example: Power analysis	Meet on Monday, January 15th	A biostatistician	Sample size
Request electronic health record data	Monday, March 15th	Me and Info Systems contact	Clear expectations on data acquisition
Example: Final interpretation of findings	Tuesday, May 20th	Me, Advisor, Statistician	Draft findings, data visualizations

TEMPLATE 13. PLAN NARRATIVE:
ASSEMBLING THE DOCUMENT

COMPONENT SIX: SCHEDULING TASKS

Step 1. Right now, as you picture your project in your mind, draw <u>a flowchart of how you envision the research project steps, stages or phases, and activities occurring</u>. This helps think about exactly what you will do to conduct and complete the project.

Step 2. In the table on the next page, make a list of tasks, timelines, and contacts to finalize your project plan, and to conduct and complete the project.

Instructions: You may need to begin at the end, when you are finished with your report, and work backwards to ensure you have allocated enough time to complete the project.

Be very detailed. You can't have too much detail in your schedule. Glitches and obstacles can occur.

You don't need as much detail in your final project plan document, but you need to have considered every action and reaction.

Include the purpose, when you will do it, who will be involved, and your expected result.

You can use this same spreadsheet to plan your activities to organize the project plan as well as to conduct it.

About the Author

Dr. dès Anges Cruser has a doctorate in interdisciplinary studies, and a master's degree in public healthcare administration. Her doctoral dissertation explored the extent to which the communications styles of teams supported or obstructed the achievement of intended program outcomes, in hospital and community behavioral health settings. She began her career after college as a U.S. Navy Officer on the staff at NATO. Following her forty-year career in healthcare systems, she worked as a consultant on innovation projects for healthcare delivery and outcomes evaluation. In every position she held in public systems, she invested herself in the success of her students in the fields of social work, psychology, physical therapy, nursing, medicine, and healthcare policy. She has conducted leadership seminars for large health-related organizations, and published and presented scientific papers internationally. It was her work in research education that inspired this book. Her full CV can be found at ResearchProject-Help.com.